ALBERT T. MURPHY is Professor of Special
Education, Communicative Disorders, and
Rehabilitation Medicine at Boston University,
where he has also been Director of the
Psycho-Educational Clinic, the Speech and
Hearing Center, and Chairman of the Division of
Special and Counselor Education. A licensed
clinical psychologist, he has written over sixty
professional publications, including several books
and monographs concerned with handicapped
children and their families.

ALBERT T. MURPHY

SPECIAL CHILDREN, SPECIAL PARENTS

Personal Issues with Handicapped Children

A SPECTRUM BOOK

PRENTICE-HALL, INC., Englewood Cliffs, N.J. 07632

Library of Congress Cataloging in Publication Data

Murphy, Albert T
    Special children, special parents.

    A Spectrum Book
    Includes index.
        1. Handicapped children—Family relationships.
    2. Handicapped children—Care and treatment.
    I. Title.
    HV888.M87   362.8′2   80–22522
    ISBN 0–13–826412–0
    ISBN 0–13–826404–X (pbk.)

*To Terry, Liz, Lou,
Van, Lee, my students,
Sylvia, Brian and Pan*

A SPECTRUM BOOK

Printed in the United States of America

10 9 8 7 6 5 4 3 2 1

PRENTICE-HALL INTERNATIONAL, INC., *London*
PRENTICE-HALL OF AUSTRALIA, PTY. LIMITED, *Sydney*
PRENTICE-HALL OF CANADA, LTD., *Toronto*
PRENTICE-HALL OF INDIA PRIVATE LIMITED, *New Delhi*
PRENTICE-HALL OF JAPAN, INC., *Tokyo*
PRENTICE-HALL OF SOUTHEAST ASIA PTE LTD., *Singapore*
WHITEHALL BOOKS LIMITED, *Wellington, New Zealand*

CONTENTS

PREFACE

This is a very personal and even a sentimental journal; its particular focus is parents of children having special needs with whom I have associated in my clinical work. I have long wished to express my gratitude to them in a tangible way for contributing so much to my education. This book constitutes my effort to fulfill that wish.

I hope that parents, professionals, and others who read this book will find that it "rings true," that while personal it is also grounded in the concrete reality of the daily family and work settings wherein special children exist, struggle, and grow. These passages flow from close contact over many years with families having children with various special needs, and thus reflect much diversity along the spectrum of experiences such families encounter. I describe these experiences from a fully subjective perspective. I have not tried to edit out my own basic feelings and attitudes. There are no academic discussions, no references to research or authority. There is only one person's perspective—my own view of the world of handicapped, problem, or ill children, their families, and those who seek to serve them, as I have experienced this world. And, although I will be attempting to convey the felt experience of professional workers, the larger purpose of this work is to convey experience from the parent's perspective.

Parents of children with special needs often feel alone in their quest for meaning and happiness in their lives. In one sense, however, no parent is ultimately alone; each is "one" with all other parents in that each shares to some degree what others experience. This common ground of interactions with special children ranges from anguished frustration to exquisite tenderness, from moments of despair to those of joy, from the deadly serious to the ridiculous, from feeling pulled apart to feeling whole. I have addressed myself to the thoughts and feelings which are often below the surface or which rise to the surface in the dark of night—the anguished, peaceful, or problem-solving solitudes of individual experience—and to the view of life as a groping toward greater understanding and an effort to create ourselves continuously, to evolve most fully through fruitful relationships with others.

Among assumptions I make about the human condition—especially those conditions connected to impairment—at least two deserve mention: (1) each and every human being has a natural drive to grow and a developmentally inclined interest in the world outside self, an interest that goes beyond mere existence or simple survival; and, (2) each and every human being has natural tendencies both toward higher levels of human functioning and toward higher levels of being-in-relationship with others. Such assumptions are challenged again and again by all concerned from the moment each realizes that a special need exists. I have charted this book's course from the moment of first awareness, the "beginning," through those key phases of the journey which frequently follow: the "holding on," the need to get one's bearings; and then, at least partially, the acceptance that a special condition exists; finally, the full calling forth of the caring response, followed by the challenges to our faith, what we believe, our doubts and trusts, what we hope for. I then consider the crucial importance of communicating openly and honestly with others and with oneself, of risking certain deep emotional investments in personal relationships where a special human condition exists. I try to share the sense of heightened learning, love, and happiness that can emerge from life with a special child—sometimes in relationship to others, but other times in chosen solitude. The overall view I present is that, in spite of misfortune, life can be full and good.

We human beings are capable of incomparable intelligence; on the other hand we also can act more stupidly and cruelly than the dumbest and fiercest of the so-called beasts. Always, however, there is the human potential for magnificence, of being fully creative. The power to create—to invent ourselves and to contribute to the actualization of another—exists in each soul. We most create ourselves in a helping relationship with another, and this is especially true in relationships with children having special needs.

The primary mental image I have experienced throughout this work is of Michaelangelo's *Captives,* in the Galleria Academia in Florence. Partly free and recognizably human, partly imprisoned in the marble mass, those partially completed figures struggle endlessly through time to achieve a full human shape. The uncarved image, like a divine spark, lies in each person, waiting for form. It is those not yet fully formed figures, children with special needs, who are represented to me by this image. Parents and workers are sculptors, helping to shape what a child may become. There is a place for all—a place to be, to become something more than they now are, a place to learn, to dance, to sing. This is every person's right, and the special child must not be forgotten. In the words of Henry Van Dyke, "The woods would be silent if no birds sang except those who sing best." This book celebrates adults and the special children with whom they coexist in the song of life, the dance of life—partners in the creative process that, given time, will bring human potentialities to form.

A.T.M.

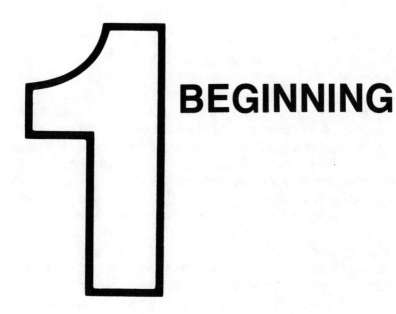

1 BEGINNING

Be willing to have it so. Acceptance
of what has happened is the first
step in overcoming the consequences
of any misfortune.

William James

1

Where should one begin? At the beginning, of course—but where was, and what was, the beginning? Was it that deeply and subtly felt, yet not consciously aware, moment of first sensing that something was not quite right? Or was it really the all too fully conscious moment of being told directly that the child was handicapped? It was one thing to be afraid that there was something wrong; it was quite another to be told point blank that something indeed was wrong. Oh, but it was too shocking, too numbing, to think straight, to realize, to grasp its proper significance. For a time all else following would be tumultuous feeling, confused thought, anger, doubt, disbelief, rage. For a time all would be numbed response rather than planned coping. Nothing would truly begin until the fact had been accepted. Acceptance would be the beginning.

With words such as these have I imagined what parents throughout time have experienced upon learning that their child is not completely normal: "Why did this happen to me?" This question, where parents of children with special problems are concerned, surely must be one of the most common. "Why did *I* have a handicapped child, and *they* have normal ones?"

I recall one group that consisted of mothers and grandmothers of hearing-impaired infants. The participants were discussing this very question. "Gramma" Allen had listened for a long time this particular evening before speaking. "There is no good answer to that question," she said, quietly but firmly, "and there never can be. This thing doesn't make sense rationally, but your job is to make sense out of it and thus bring about your own answer. That is your responsibility, and that is your opportunity." Not all who heard Gramma Allen that night could heed the advice. There are moments when we can put thought and feeling into action, but there are others when we cannot. Author Pearl Buck, whose own daughter was retarded, wrote eloquently of this in *The Child Who Never Grew.* She encouraged each parent to remember that the child has a right to life, whatever that life may be, and the right to happiness:

This child has a meaning for you and for all children. You will find a job you cannot suspect in fulfilling his life for and with him. Lift up your head and go your appointed way.*

Each child, first-born or last, handicapped or not, means something special to its parents. Nobody expects to become the parent of a handicapped child. Our expectations are of quite a different kind, and they sometimes die very hard.

My wife would not accept the fact of Susan's deafness. Our school had a policy of having the kids wear their hearing aids on top of their clothing. But Phyllis found every excuse to hide Susan's aid. She even got to the point of making a heart-shaped, lace trimmed harness for the aid, then a different harness for every outfit. It got ridiculous.

How hard it often is to accept one's child or one's life as it is, rather than how one would wish it to be. But acceptance of reality is the key that unlocks the potentials for creative adjustment.

Yet, there is shock, anguish, numbness. This cannot have happened. But it has. It is no dream.

*Pearl S. Buck, *The Child Who Never Grew* (New York: John Day Co., 1950), p. 59.

We thought she would be the prettiest and the smartest. We looked forward to being with her, helping her to become a fine woman. There would be fun along the way—playful times together. Why would we give a thought to brain-damage?

Yes, I think of the boy he might have been, the things he would have seen were he not blind: birds flying, beautiful flowers, his mother's smiling face. And then I wonder why this had to happen. I'm sure I'm not alone in wondering this way.

And there is guilt, the feeling of guilt because occasionally you feel as though the child you wanted had died—and the child you were never prepared for came instead. You wonder what the child you longed for would have been like. Unusual thoughts? Not at all. Endless numbers of parents have experienced such wonderment before—and will experience it forever after us. It was the ancient Roman, Marcus Aurelius, who said that everything that happens, happens as it should, and if you observe carefully you will find this to be so.

And yet, to accept is not necessarily to become reconciled to the problem. Can we ever fully accept the unacceptable? We adjust to reality. Life may not be complete, yet we need not accept less than we must. As one parent said:

When my mind is at rest, and my senses are stilled, then I accept the fact that whatever happens, it is natural, it is according to nature's law.

In life, no one is truly greater, or truly less. Consider this sixteenth-century quotation:

Nothing imperfect is;
Equal are gold and tin.
Frogs are as beautiful
As the seraphim.

Whatever *is* warrants its own significance by mere existence. That is the wondrous and equal reality.

An image comes to my mind; a memory of a young mother of a child born with a severe cleft palate and harelip, a child easily recognizable by others as different. The mother is still angry over her ill fate. She hands me a little card on which are printed these words: "God created man in his own image, in the image of God created He him" (*Genesis,* 1:27). "What a laugh," she cries. "What kind of image do you call that face? What God would do that? Or does God have a harelip?" At such times perhaps one can only listen quietly and try to be fully present to the other. For some the burden is heavy, in-comprehensible, seemingly endless.

But the kind of rueful acceptance that is fixated at the level of mere suffering does nothing for our emotional health and renders us less capable of being all that we could be—for ourselves and others. It rather hardens us in a stoical way. Brute acceptance or suffering has no value of its own. The suffering itself needs sharing, although in an ultimate sense we do suffer alone. In its most unbearable moments, in the most deeply personal experiences, we sense the futility of trying to have others understand. Even when sympathy is expressed, it often seems inadequate. But endless suffering, which may be in great part self-maintained, does no good. In fact, there is an odd and unfortunate added feature to such suffering that suggests martydom. In the eyes of friends and relatives who may listen with kindness to the parental declarations of injus-tice and sorrow, the litany eventually becomes simply *boring,* with all of the sorry consequences boredom brings.

I knew I needed to do something when one day I asked my favorite brother why he seldom visited us anymore. He didn't pull any punches either. He looked me straight in the eye, pointed his finger at me and said, "Look. With you it's problems and nothing but problems. So you have a retarded child. I feel for you, and I want to help, I really do. But, honest, it's just gotten terribly *boring*—and *you've* gotten terribly boring—there *are* other things in the world beside *your problems*. I've got a few of my own. But there's more to life. If you could start paying some attention to the things beyond yourself—the other things that should be a part of your life, not just your problems, we'd all be a lot better off—a lot happier—and then we'd see more of each other. But I'm sick of your sadness, and bored with it, too."

The old adage is still wise in such situations: Do not put all of your eggs in one basket. St. Augustine stated the same idea in this way: "Do not let your entire happiness depend on something you may lose."

In deep suffering, our courage and our ability to spring back are severely tested. How can we face it? What will we do? Yet even these questions have a hopeful aspect to them; they reflect an orientation toward the future, an attitude toward action. Suffering reminds us of our human fallibility, our inevitable aloneness. But suffering shared with another, expressed to another in any form, is a step in the right direction. No matter how difficult it is for the other to comprehend completely, this sharing can become part of a life-growth experience. Suffering may need solitude, but it always needs communion.

Full acceptance requires some pain; perhaps there really is no coming to full awareness about *any* important dimension of life without pain. In life's emotional storms, there is no overcoming without undergoing. And always there is this truth: To overcome misfortune we must *first* accept the fact that it exists.

A Yiddish proverb says that each child carries his own blessing into the world. But it is sometimes hard to see a blessing through tears or to hear it above the shouts of rage at what has happened.

The worst part of my anger and pain is the feeling of *helplessness*. I feel *helpless!* With no rhyme or reason suddenly you

have lost part of your life—things have gotten out of control, out of your own hands.

It is one of life's ironies that at just those times when we feel our worst we must try to do our best. Yet life repeatedly suggests to us that it must have meaning. Our purpose in living is to discover that meaning and live in accord with it. We have, then, something to live for.

It has been said that the greatest thing you can do when you are depressed is to learn something. It is no minor lesson to learn this; for life to assume meaning, one approach is to simply *do* something rather than resign or accept passively. In the concentration camps of World War II, it was a common sight to see those who were still able to rally around others who were utterly depressed and giving up; the able ones would taunt, deride, or anger those whose hope had waned, would do anything to get them onto their feet, to react, to simply *do* something, anything relating to a current or future task such as helping another. The doing could bring a meaning to their difficult condition. It was often found in those wretched circumstances that suffering ceases to be suffering per se the moment it finds meaning. In part, of course, it is a matter of taking the right attitude, as difficult as the challenge may be, or seeing the situation from an altered perspective. The magnificent Helen Keller once said that if you keep your face to the sunshine, you will not see the shadow.

Each person has the possibility of experiencing the gravely stirring realization that is the perverse quality of tragedy; it describes what is now possible. We do not choose some things. They choose us, and increasingly our lives are less our own. Yet many have made a further discovery: that only in losing your life in another do you truly find yourself.

Crises are a part of all living. It is deadly to become mired in hurt or anger or self-pity. Self-pity immobilizes, draws away energy. To grow it is necessary to *do,* to set up some positive activity, however small it may seem; to turn away occasionally from the narrowed focus of a problem area; to turn not away from everything else, but toward other interests, other people. Isolation deadens.

In some instances, of course, it is the handicapped person, not others, who has the greatest challenge to accept what has happened. One father relates this incident:

There was Peter, a healthy fourteen-year-old athlete, and all of a sudden there was the diving accident, a broken neck, and lying on the Stryker frame with tongs in his head and heavy traction weights, and being turned every two hours. God, it was awful! Then one day a young man rolled happily into the ward in his wheelchair and started talking about how he was driving his own car and dating girls at college. He talked with Peter a long time, and toward the end he said, "You realize you may never walk again."

I cried a lot that night, and I'm sure Peter did, too. But from that day on he had a new, more cooperative attitude toward the whole rehabilitation program.

Initial acceptance, once it has occurred, is a victory. But there are other acceptances that must be faced. The family and the child will need to work through acceptance at various times. Far ahead, perhaps, will be the need to accept and work through the challenges of educational and vocational worlds. In between is the repeated acceptance of the difference, temporary or permanent, between a handicapped child and others more fortunate. Crisis periods are encountered by all families and each individual. Some we experience in common: moving from one neighborhood to another, the illness or death of or separation from loved ones. Others may be special to the child with a special need: the need for medical treatment, special services, or possible institutionalization. For all family members there are adjustments to one another, departures, marriages, divorces, births. At each critical point, each family member needs to work toward adjustment, acceptance. And each crisis can be an incapacitating or a cohesive force, both within the family and within each individual. The mother of a quadriplegic cerebral-palsied girl once wrote these words:

Because of handicaps, not every child can run or walk, hit a baseball, see the stars in the night sky, or hear the song of a meadowlark. But every child can know the feel of wind in her hair, or warm rain on her face, the coolness of shade beneath the oak, the touch of running water and the cool moss that lies alongside. Yes, I see myself more clearly in the light of their innocence.

THE LEGEND OF ATHENA

There are times in everyone's life when nothing seems to go right. Every parent of a handicapped child knows this, but so does every parent and person in the world. There are times when we seem singled out by a malicious fate. Others may tell us that having difficulties is part of the human condition, but when we are deeply distressed, we probably feel that we have had more than our share. It is at such moments that I recall the legend of Athena and the box of olive wood. It seems that on the Acropolis above Athens there was a shrine dedicated to the goddess Athena. On a certain day each year the Athenians visited the shrine. On the altar rested an open box made of olive wood, and into this box all citizens were allowed to deposit a scroll upon which all of their troubles and sorrows had been written. One may imagine the blessing this could be! However, there was a proviso—as one might suspect. In depositing your problems it was required that you carry away someone else's. We can guess what happened: After reading the scrolls of others, each person went home with his own.

No life lacks pain, but no life lacks meaning either. The *living* provides the meaning—even though, in the final analysis, it has to be for each of us the meaning that each of us *gives* it. In whatever form, the end of life is *life*. And life is a state of action, the full use of our power; this is our responsibility and this is our joy. Think about what Camus has said: "In the middle of winter I discovered that I carried within me an invincible summer." Hear. Accept. Go on!

None of us can prevent misfortune
from striking. But we can determine
our attitude toward the unkind
shafts of fate.

Gordon Allport (Pattern and Growth in Personality
[New York: Holt, Rinehart and Winston, 1961], p. 561).

SURVIVING

OVERCOMING THROUGH UNDERGOING

One finally realizes that the first step in overcoming a problem is to admit that it exists. How common it is to deny the reality of a handicapping condition! The pain is difficult to bear, at least for a time. And perhaps, in a true sense, the difficulty is never completely accepted. Rather, it is in part adjusted to, compensated for, woven into the fabric of the whole cloth of one's life.

When they told us she was mongoloid I just went into a kind of shock, I guess. Everything they told me I heard, but it didn't register—or maybe it did deep inside me. For a few days I just hung on like a sailor in a storm—not thinking, just keeping afloat. Gradually it sunk in.

In the period immediately following the realization of the handicap, a kind of numbed hanging on frequently occurs. This initial endurance of unavoidable sorrow, a feat in itself, is a beginning. For what is accepted requires enduring—the hanging on while working through. Adjustment and reintegration will occur—not suddenly, but little by little. One father of a blind girl, who had resolutely refused any responsibility for her care, finally was able to say, "Yes, she is blind and that's final. But now I know that life does go on. It must. Her blindness actually has changed nothing except myself. Now I must think beyond myself for her sake."

No one is to be excused from life—any of it—its joys *or* its sorrows: the dark day of discovery; the changes brought to life's patterns; the wrenching realizations and the visions of hope; the self-pity, the grieving, the recognitions, the understandings, the resolutions; old dreams broken and newer dreams forming; disbeliefs, denials; the hard work and the play; the crying and laughter; the dry details of daily coping; the moments of joy shared. No one is excused.

My husband wouldn't admit for a long time that Jimmy wasn't normal. But you can't deny these things forever. That's useless. It's worse than useless, it's destructive. It hurt our relationship. Then I saw that how we behaved set the pattern for the whole family. Now, through our talking things out at the clinic here, and more and more at home, we're turning things around. But you can't be an ostrich about these things. They're too important to blind yourself to them. Too many things are affected, too many people—yourself most of all.

Many parents of handicapped children have believed that the relationship as parent with child is less complete because of the handicap than it would otherwise have been. The following statements suggest this sense of loss or frustration in the limits set by the handicap on the parent-child relationship: "There is so much unsaid." "There is so much to be said." "It is so hard to say what must be said." And, "There is so much not done." "It is so hard to do what has to be done." "It is so hard to know what should be done."

GUILT, ANGER, AND THE UNEXPECTED GIFT

For some parents, to endure and to accept mean to endure and accept the guilt they feel. Perhaps they begin with the general proposition that the good are rewarded, the evil punished; then they deduce the particular: "We suffer because we must be guilty—of something."

The usual situation, of course, is that whatever causes exist to create the handicap usually are beyond parental control. In any situation, guilt makes no real contribution to the care and happiness of the child. It weakens the unifying and creative energies of the parent, sets up an undesirable model of behavior for the rest of the family, and generally interferes with the development of a healthy relationship with the special child and of the child's own personality.

Inappropriate guilt must be relinquished. Positive future-oriented outlooks must be nurtured. For a time there may be guilt, however, and not infrequently it is mixed with anger. The mother of a boy born without limbs, in a recent letter to me, wrote the following:

All my wishful thinking! All my "if onlys"! My hopes for relief. My thoughts of abandoning him. My frequent feelings of not caring, feeling guilty, the shame and embarrassment, and wondering who gives a damn! All those days of resentment—the extra burdens and the traveling to doctors and the feeding and dressing and washing and the sleepless nights and on and on and on. Not to mention the effect of all of this on the rest of the family. And the anger at others and mostly at myself for having such thoughts—and the horrible feelings of guilt. . . . But now, after these many months, I have come to realize that I'm not alone in thinking and feeling the way I did. I've discovered that just about every parent of a child born with a handicap—especially a serious one—has these experiences for a time. And even more than that, I realize now that it isn't even unusual for parents of *normal* children to have these kinds of thoughts once in a while.

Funny, but in all of this I've somehow gotten stronger myself as a person. As though my son's disorder were a special kind of lens that has allowed me to see—mankind, really—all people, better. It dawned on me recently that I'm much less judgmental of others—no matter who they are or what they do. I understand more. I have no right to judge them, certainly not to condemn them. Somehow, through my son, I've come to feel something of what many others feel that I could never feel before. No, it was not easy at first, but the struggle has brought me some dividends I never dreamed existed. A kind of gift you might say.

We are not surprised that a parent should sometimes feel like a solitary, defiant warrior fighting fate—wanting to live life fully but raging against it at the same time. It can seem that there is, indeed, little to celebrate. The struggle endures, however, for many reasons, perhaps even because sometimes we delude ourselves. For all our pains and failures, our misery and our petty irritations, from time to time—and often when we least expect it—a divine (or even devilish) spark ignites our spirit, causing us to rise above it all. And then just being here seems important. And all of this caring, all of these chores seem to require us and, oddly, we give ourselves purposefully to them. We have brought ourselves to a moment of personal creativity through a caring relationship with another.

The caring relationship must not be merely one of endless chores. Dedication without self-realization is not creative; indeed, it may be the suffocation of the creative impulse. When it leads to feelings of unbearable sacrifice, we have entered into martyrdom and stagnation.

One must persist beyond brute endurance. The struggle may not be easy. The mother of a multiply handicapped child said, "I'm in double jeopardy. I not only grieve; I think incessantly about my grieving." Another parent admitted, "I fear; I hesitate; I blame; I even envy others. But I can overcome most of this. Some of it is just normal." Author Herman Hesse once said, "It is easy to underestimate the sufferings of others. It is even easier to overestimate the happiness of others."

"Where do you get your strength to go on?" the mother of a dying girl was asked by members of our counseling group. "You not only go on," they said, "but you do so cheerfully. What is your secret weapon?" Her reply: "I don't need a weapon against her death because I don't believe in death, only the fear of death. And the fear can be dealt with."

Guilt can be dealt with. Anger can be dealt with. Fear, envy, doubts, and all of the other emotions of living can be dealt with. But *not* through denial. *Not* through experiencing them only privately. And *not* through experiencing them so that their effects are unkind to oneself or to others. All may be dealt with best by recognizing their presence and working through them in relationship with others, and in a few quiet times of self-searching solitude.

It doesn't comfort me that other parents have a similar misfortune. It does comfort me, however, to see that others have coped, have learned to live with their heartache, and go beyond it. Perhaps it was at this point that I turned the corner to full acceptance.

The mother of two children, both severely handicapped, once spoke these words to me:

As a young wife, I dreamed of having two things—healthy children and a beautiful garden. I now have a lovely garden, but my dream of a healthy child has not come true. The lovely garden of healthy children has so far been denied us, perhaps is locked to us forever. And yet each of our children has brought us special joys. As the poster in your office says, "A single rose can be my garden."

We may not have thought of disability. We may not have chosen it. But we can choose how to respond to it. In so choosing, we can discover personal strengths unimagined, relationships of tremendous reward, and ways to invent ourselves to derive the most out of life, and to bring the most to it. A young man with cerebral palsy with whom I occasionally attend sporting events said to me one evening, "How like a cloud passing by this life is—each one of us just once—and never another time. But our having been here—doesn't that leave somehow an everlasting trace?" We looked at each other and smiled, as though we both answered, "Yes, it does."

CARING 3

The joys of parents are secret:
and so are their griefs and fears.
They cannot utter the one;
nor they will not utter the other.
Children sweeten labors, but they
make misfortunes more bitter.
They increase the cares of life,
but they mitigate the remembrance
of death.

Sir Francis Bacon, Essays

19

Love, broadly speaking, manifests itself as care. As Milton Mayeroff, in his compassionate and helpful book, *On Caring,* has observed, to care for another person is to help the other to grow, to self-actualize, to achieve potentials in the largest measure. Caring includes a deep respect for the other. It assumes that an impaired child needs to grow and has the capacity to grow in a unique way. To care is also to feel needed and to respond to that need, whether it is in respect to a parent and child, teacher and pupil, counselor and patient, or husband and wife. Each caring relationship contains within it the nurturing that helps the other to grow. In true caring or love we have the quintessential example of mutually creative relationship. Every act of selfless devotion, of care or love, enriches us. All of the wise through the ages have known this secret. Love alone brings authentic happiness. In the deep heart's core, each parent—each of us—knows this to be so.

According to Rainer Maria Rilke, each of us will carry forth from the earth a single word or phrase, like "fruit tree" or "fountain." Each of us will bring with us the word we loved most (and also a sprig of blue or yellow gentians). For many, the word will be "love" or "caring." For parents of impaired children, the caring will need to occur across a wide span of day-by-day time. But caring manifests itself from a variety of human sources and can occur even in transitory encounters.

I recall a scene that occurred in one of our clinics recently. All of the children in that particular group had severe learning disabilities. A group of adult visitors was passing through, and one of them wondered aloud what time it was. We could see Timmy look at the desk clock and grimace in his silent calculations. But before Timmy could answer, one of the other visitors did. Timmy frowned and walked away. A third visitor, however, had noticed the incident and a minute later "accidentally" strolled past Timmy and asked if anyone knew the time. Another grimace preceded Timmy's accurate response. "Thank you," the visitor said, "I'm glad you were here to help." "It's O.K.," he replied, looking with pride at his teacher. At that moment, all three were smiling in the glow of the creative act of a gracious and caring person.

A caring response is a gift from any source, and in some situations it is particularly appropriate and appreciated:

After having a child with Tay-Sacks disease, I was naturally anxious about my next pregnancy. My pediatrician on his own telephoned me a few times and was very encouraging and supportive. I was extremely fortunate to have such a person.

This mother, who was also a junior high school teacher, once told me that one of her sources of peace and comfort was G. K. Chesterton's view that the way to love anything is to realize that it may be lost. How true this seems!

Each of us not only has needs, but we have a need to be needed. We do not envy the person who is not needed, for that individual is incomplete, unfulfilled. We are able to create ourselves fully only when we have available to us supportive relationships. Such relationships are two-way streets—we search not only for what we ourselves lack, but also for what we are needed for. In healthy relationships we not only receive sufficient love or care, we are enabled to care for, to give love. In such ways we actuate ourselves as we actuate others. The more I care, and act upon my caring, the happier I seem to be, the more I transcend self-absorption, become something more than I was. In one way, to help another to survive and grow is to experience the other as an extension of myself, myself as an extension of them. I am part of the other; the other is part of me. I think here not only of how important to growth parents are to children, and professionals may be to parents, but also of how frequently some parents are crucial to the growth of professionals.

Dr. Albert Schweitzer, in a talk to the students of a school in England in 1935, made this statement: "I do not know what your destiny will be. But I know one thing: the only ones among you who will be really happy are those who have sought and found how to serve."

And yet, it is sometimes so difficult to care, to continue caring, to continue to care and really mean it.

Sometimes I find myself silently cursing the unfairness of it all. I know I'm not alone in this feeling. And I'm a religious person. But I still sense a deep bitterness within me for my child and others like him. I know I will never understand why this had to be. Oh, I know the facts—even the medical facts and the theory—but my feelings drown out the facts. Still, it's not my mind that gives me the strength to continue caring and doing, it's something in my heart.

For most, to care is to be carried—beyond oneself—toward and into the life of another, and to realize at some level of awareness that the meaning one has to fulfill in life is, indeed, *beyond* oneself; it is never *merely* oneself.

But, again, what if there is little or no response to my giving? What if the response is less than I need, or expect? I may get upset, angry, disappointed—with the child, my friend, my husband, myself. Then I feel unworthy—guilty—and I end up depressed. Many have said this sort of thing to me. One, the mother of a retarded deaf boy, had sunk to a point of despair but gained renewed hope when the mother of a dying girl spoke these words to her:

You feel a deep sorrow, but you can do something about it; what if he were suffering and you couldn't do anything about it? May you never experience that. You are too focused on yourself. You can't bear life if you cut yourself off from it. Shift yourself out of keeping to yourself. Look to things beyond yourself. You'll see that you can bear the hurt and rise above it. Not without some pain, you know, but rise above it you will. You can. You must!

Anne Morrow Lindbergh, in *Gift from the Sea,* speaks of women instinctively wanting to give, yet resenting giving themselves in small pieces—the myriad details of housekeeping, family routine, and child care. What a woman most deeply resents is not so much the giving of herself in pieces as in giving herself purposelessly. Purposeful giving belongs to the natural order of things; it is not apt to deplete one's resources—the more one gives, the more one has to give—like milk in the breast.

Every parent wants to be the "magical teacher"—one whose irresistible and enlightening touch the child awaits and who causes the beauty of the child to flower. Some professionals indulge in this hope, too. Before success comes the image of success, before compassion tenderness, before the child's growth caring. To paraphrase Goethe, in praising or loving or teaching a child, we praise and love and teach not that which is, but that which we hope for. Our caring will manifest itself not only in attitude but in action taken—in assisting, encouraging, and helping the child *also* to become a caring person. In caring for others, he will become more independently functioning and more self-determining.

Sometimes, it is true, a parent will reveal a caring that is overbearing, perhaps to the point of resenting other family members because they take time from "the appointed task." One mother, who had become more martyr than mother in her excessive devotion to her neurologically impaired child, finally realized what she was doing through the caring but honest reaction of friends. She at last concluded that her first task was to keep a happy home, that the family's rights included *her* responsibility to be happy and in relationship with all of them, that her handicapped son would have to take his place in the total picture. "We cannot always fit ourselves to his limitations," she concluded, "and the world never would." We are reminded here that one of the classical virtues is *prudence,* which is founded on the recognition that doing good assumes a sound knowledge of reality, that simply "meaning well" is not enough.

The cared-for child cannot be allowed to dominate the other family members. Nor can the parents seek to possess or dominate him. It is rather a matter of trying to be present to the other with an open heart and mind, open to the thoughts and feelings, open to the possibilities, open to the risks that are part of any deeply felt investment of oneself in another. It is a matter of caring enough to risk allowing the child to guide us, recognizing that we are shaped by his behavior as surely as he is shaped by ours.

I recall Mr. P., whose son, a second grader, was showing many of the characteristics typical of learning-impaired children—reading disability, writing and spelling errors, left/right hand and direction confusion. The father had resisted full participation in our counseling group, claiming that the responsibility for helping the child was mainly his wife's, and also that he couldn't really get the boy to behave the way he wanted him to. Mr. P.'s hobby was watercolor painting. One evening I asked him if he would comment on a well-known phrase, "The material creates the artist." Among other things, he said, that "the artist lets the object of his study suggest to him how to appreciate and develop." I asked him if a parent could be thought of as an artist in relation to his children. He allowed that it could be the case. He realized that much of the refinement of an artist's vision occurs as he works toward realizing his creation through interaction with his "materials," and he was then able to relate this to his role, responsibility, and opportunities with his son. The analogy served also to clarify that the quality of an effort to be creative depends on the material, the tools, and the artist's hand whose movements they subtly control. This led to a realization that his son was being much more effective in shaping the father's behavior than the father was in shaping the son's. With increased awareness stemming from a perspective that was meaningful and interesting to him, Mr. P. went on to take a much more active and mutually enhancing part in the life of his son.

Caring has most potential for the good when it is somehow responsive to the deeper needs, curiosities, wishes, or fantasies of those involved. One must care, and still learn to care even more. Patience will be a virtue. Some confusion and anguish will serve to threaten our caring. At some such times it will be important to remember to care sufficiently for *oneself,* also. We, ourselves, deserve opportunity to take care of and be responsive to our own needs. We must respect our own persons enough to have confidence in the necessary decisions we must make every day; to have faith in our ability to learn, not only from our mistakes, but from the one cared for as well. This view, I believe, holds as true for teachers, counselors, and other workers as it does for parents.

"But how much is expected of me?" asked one parent. "How much am I expected to give?" One of my colleagues answered: "You can only give what you have to give, but you have to give all of it." Another continued: "I'm not sure I would agree. I'm afraid too many parents feel that they have to give it all, and when they feel angry or resentful about this they really can get into some painful self-punishment. When that happens, everybody bleeds!" Perhaps we could say that caring fully for another is not possible unless we also care for our own well-being; when I care for myself in a healthy way, I am better able to show care for another.

I sing to the ears that are
stopped, the eyes that are
sealed, and the minds that do not labor.*

James Stephens (*The Crock of Gold* [New York:
Collier Books, 1967], p. 114).

4 CREATING

They live most happily who most fully invent themselves. We ourselves are our greatest invention. To invent ourselves is to make of ourselves something more than we are—in short, to grow. The most remarkable growths of self occur, for most of us, through positive relationships with others—our mothers or fathers, our sisters and brothers, our husbands or wives, our own children and grandchildren, our teachers, our friends, and co-workers.

Parents may invent themselves through their relationships with each other and with their children. Parents "make" children, but children have the capacity of "making" their parents, because they change the particular vision parents have of the world and of themselves. This leads parents to modifications of their customary ways of behaving, in other words to a *transformation*. Such occurrences provide opportunities for creating ourselves in a loving and helping relationship with another. We are often unconscious of these creative moments. They are often not intentional, not willed, yet they emerge again and again. The mother of a boy whose face had been deeply scarred in a fire once said, "God does not create in order to get something, but in order to give something—and we feel the same way."

The father of a boy with muscular dystrophy said this:

The major problems in life are never completely figured out. And, let's face it, you could think of a handicapped child as a problem. But why that problem picks you, and what sense and purpose you can get out of it, well, that is what I keep working at. I hope for an answer, and in my own way I work to get it—but getting the answer turns out to be not the important thing—it's the working out of things that really keeps us going—and I guess that gives it all a meaning—and a purpose.

THE BASIC URGE TO FULLER HUMANNESS AS A UNIVERSAL LIFE FORCE

I believe that each individual has a natural need to be in a mutually nurturing relationship with others. This is the case no matter how impaired the child, his parents, or their relationship. Twenty-five years of counseling parents of children with a wide variety of disorders have done nothing to shake my belief that parents, at the bottom line, want to become something more than they are, both as individuals and in relationship with their family members and others. There have naturally been times when this belief has been severely challenged, as in the case of a child-batterer, or a father who as punishment held his children's hands over gas-stove flames, or others who abused their children in even more horrifying ways. It has been very difficult for me in such instances to avoid rejecting the person while abhorring the action. However, in every case in which I had the opportunity to come to know such a parent more completely, when I had the opportunity to learn of their frustrations and hurts, my appreciation grew for their particular way of struggling to be human. Many a cry of anger has been but a disguised cry for love and the desire to feel oneself to be a person of some worth.

Improvement in living—between parent and child or between any two people—is a *creative* event. Improvement in one's own life or relationships—toward total functioning—is frequently a movement from habituated but nondevelopmental security toward insecurity—creative insecurity. To grow is to invent, to create oneself. In *person*-oriented relationships—in therapy, education, or social settings—both parties have an opportunity to invent themselves. Each grows by choosing, by taking responsibility, becoming free to risk, in *not* simply being safe. Apply this to the child; apply it to the clinician or teacher; apply it to parents. The point is expressed in a lovely way on an ancient tablet on the coast of Greece:

A shipwrecked sailor buried on this coast
Bids you set sail;
Full many a bark, when we were lost,
Weathered the gale.

For those seeking to serve, work at its best is a process of creating self through a helping relationship with others. Some people perceive this as selfish; yet is this not but *growth*-oriented self-interest in the best sense, an interest in self-improvement that may lead to more productive functioning with others? The wisdom of the ages speaks to us of these matters. We cannot exist for ourselves alone.

The eminent theologian, Martin Buber, distinguished between two attitudes toward others: (1) The *I-Thou* relationship is one of direct, mutual openness, of being fully present with the other and, with an open heart, of intimate person-to-person encounter; (2) The *I-It* relationship is depersonalized, detached. Whenever we come into the presence of others with interest and without regarding them as objects, items, or instruments to be used for some end, we are personally involved and the *I-Thou* relationship holds. Where parents of handicapped children are concerned, as with all optimal human relationships, the ideal and the act are I-Thou based. Herein lies the foundation for mutual creativity, for mutual activation, for going beyond the self.

One of my favorite stories, one which captures the spirit of the inborn urge to realize one's potentials fully, and which I have shared in various forms with many handicapped children and their parents, is this one by Antoine de St. Exupery:

When the wild ducks or the wild geese migrate in their season, a strange tide rises in the territory over which they sweep. As if magnetized by the triangular flight, the barnyard fowl leap a foot or two into the air and try to fly. The call of the wild strikes them with the force of a harpoon and a vestige of savagery quickens their blood. All the ducks on the farm are transformed for an instant into migrant birds, and into those hard little heads, till now filled with humble images of pools and worms and barnyards, there swims a sense of continental expanse, of the breadth of seas and the salt taste of the ocean wind. The duck totters to right and left in its wire enclosure, gripped by a sudden passion to perform the impossible and a sudden love whose object is a mystery.*

Each child, each parent, is unique and deserves being recognized and treated as such. As Martin Buber observed, every person born represents something new, something that never existed, something original, unique. No two "mentally retarded" children are the same; no two "blind," "deaf," or "schizophrenic" children are; no two parents are. There are, by the way, languages in the Pacific Islands in which each and every tree on the Island has a name but there is no word for tree. To these islanders, trees are not alike. To categorize individuals by labels is to run counter to the creative impulse. Children may be trained to conform, to accept, to follow, to imitate; similarly, they may be taught to question, to examine, to create. Both children and parents may learn to think of themselves in restrictive or expansive ways, as having the capacity to be less or more able to learn. Widespread creativity *can* become a habit.

*From Antoine de Saint Exupery, *Wind, Sand and Stars*, trans. by Lewis Galantiere (New York: Harcourt Brace Jovanovitch, 1967), p. 226. Reprinted by permission.

Even if my role as "a good mother" is appreciated by others, still I often feel terribly alone. It is only when someone takes me by the hand, not as a "good parent" but in sisterhood, as a friend or lover—as one who also "searches" for life—that I exercise that deep give-and-take that strengthens my individual person—the personal. Then I truly feel like a whole person.

The scientist discovers a universal law in a grain of sand, the artist a magnificent carving imagined in a piece of driftwood, the parent a key insight about self from the presence or response of a handicapped child.

To invent oneself, to be in creative relationship with another is to go *beyond*: beyond fixed beliefs, rigid rules, routine; beyond the commonplace, the closed, the restricted, the repetitious, and the known. It is to go *toward*: toward renewal, freshness, and fullness in relationships; toward greater openness, risk, enlargement, deepening, aliveness; toward freedom, variety, experimentation, playfulness. Life should be an art—the art of creating ourselves. Life is the great gift, not for what it gives us, but because of what it allows us to give to others, and by so doing to become our finest selves.

Creative interaction tries to point up the strengths and possibilities of the present; it stresses assets more than liabilities in parents or child. It also tries to stir a sense of what is *possible* in a way that enlarges the goodness of the present in relation to an attainable future—for example, the setting up of realistic goals and the growth experience of working together to reach them.

If parents have an ultimate purpose as parents, perhaps it is, through fruitful relationships with their children, to discover their own gifts and to use them. Here, on this path, may we find our true identity—this search for self-identity may be the basic purpose behind all creative effort.

Every experience is great and mysterious. May we respect it as if it were a God walking among us in the guise of a casual stranger.

John Berry (Flight of White Crows [New York: Macmillan Co., 1961], p. 149. Reprinted by permission.)

5 BELIEVING

Many families, upon learning that a child is handicapped, are moved for a time from a settled pattern of living to one viewed as threatening to this balance. This is partly because the new circumstance tests the assumptions by which individual family members have customarily related to each other; basic perspectives have been disrupted. Sometimes this intrusion threatens even the most firmly established life outlooks, such as the religious faith of family members.

To many, faith is a belief in something that is not "known." In the Epistle to the Hebrews, faith is described as "the substance of things hoped for, the evidence of things not seen." Each parent in the world has hoped for a healthy child. If the child is not all that is hoped for, especially in extreme cases, faith may be shaken. The very principles by which one lives may be harshly challenged. Questions of the following kinds occur: "If there is a God, why did he do this?" "Why did this happen to us and not others?" "Why did this happen to such a wonderful child when all the bad ones seem to go through life unharmed?"

Disbelief, anger, and a feeling of being punished are common reactions. Some parents find themselves reacting not so much in frustration or anger but in terms of the mystery of existence. Still others become intensely aware of their unfulfilled desire for a final knowing, or for definite answers or explanations of what has happened. Some pray; others wish for miracles. A few respond with deep feelings of guilt. Not a few, for perhaps days or weeks, simply "go through the motions" required in daily living—somewhat dazed really. All are ways of responding to disappointment. All, for better or for worse, are ways of coping with one of life's shocks. Clinically speaking, all are deeply respected for the depth of humanity they represent.

Throughout each life the role of faith is an important one, and perhaps this is especially so where handicapped children and their parents are concerned. Faith in oneself, faith in one's child, and faith in the goodness and support of the family and society at large are necessary ingredients if maximum health and achievement are to occur. Not the least important of faith's characteristics is that it is *forward*-looking.

Faith is *future*-oriented. To have faith at all implies a belief in the possibility that something desired can occur. Many of the problems experienced by parents of impaired children derive from *past* unpleasant experiences, the effects of which persist into and affect their view of the present. Other problems flow from an overemphasis on *present* orientation; this is a parental inclination to do whatever is right or efficacious here-and-now but in the absence of an overarching perspective which includes past, present, and future and which does not deny the value of any of them. All have an important place in creative parental functioning—and in creative counseling, too. Not least important is the degree to which impaired children have faith in their own capacity to become something more than they are now, in terms of a specific skill or in terms of total life functioning. It is quite remarkable to see a child who has failed perhaps a thousand times suddenly accomplish a task successfully—whether it is walking without falling, speaking without stuttering, or reading without failure. It is even more remarkable to see a child who has failed try yet again. The trying must be related to a faith in a possibility, just as a lack of trying may be related to a lack of faith. It is similarly remarkable to see parents who, in the face of a child's repeated problem in adequately coping with a particular challenge, continue to participate with and provide nurturing for the child after so many disappointments. Many of us have heard words similar to these spoken by the mother of a child diagnosed as autistic:

To realize that you have given everything and that it hasn't been enough, that you have done all you could and it wasn't enough, that you weren't enough—that's more than enough. That is too much!

The faith to go on beyond such hurt must include a belief in one's own ability, not only to care for oneself but to care in a way that is responsive to one's need to care for a child. It includes, whether consciously recognized or not, a faith in one's ability to learn from experience. It is a faith that attracts one to the growth possibilities in the relationship. One mother of a severely retarded infant remarked:

I have been told the facts, and I respect those who told me the facts. But I believe in a Godly presence. I believe that faith can move mountains, and if not mountains, well then, molehills. You can tell me what you think, but I really listen to what I feel.

Faith's way of being and becoming in relationship is to move with increasing confidence into the risky known and the even more dangerous unknown. Under many life circumstances related to handicapping conditions, faiths stand in jeopardy. The parent who one day might say, "In each person, there is a divine spark, and we mean to light it," may on another day, depressed, admit, "I'm uncertain about how possible his getting better really is." Such variations in mood and outlook are hardly unusual. There is no one way to handle hurt.

I sometimes envy those who have a personal god to believe in. To them I suppose their child is a gift—*and* a test of their mettle, maybe, of their ability to be good and strong parents. Not

believing that way, we're on our own, for better or worse. But, you know, I like the idea of doing it on our own, especially if we grow stronger. No—for us, heaven and hell are right here, right now.

Another parent, a divorced mother of an adolescent paralyzed in a diving accident, made this statement:

I don't believe in doing good or being good because I might go to hell in the hereafter if I don't. I've already known hell in this life, and I discovered that I can rise above it. I believe in people.

Whatever their sources of belief in the possibilities of life, parents who live most happily and productively with their children find in these sources a strengthening love and the sanctity of human nature, along with a sense of responsibility. The wellsprings which answer our need to believe, which motivate us to live the best possible life, are all around us: each precious flower, every glorious melody, all gifts of time. In each human breast lies a deep hunger to pluck each moment as one would pluck a sweet cherry following a hard day under the hot sun.

The beliefs that enrich life are not those which wall us off from others but are, rather, expansive; they open our sympathies widely. After all, some beliefs are shadows darkening the days with fears; others are like blinders; some indeed, are like the garment of death. But the beliefs that make life worth living are like sunshine, bathing others with a happy warmth, bringing blessedness, added self-confidence and expanded feelings of personal worth—indeed, as one person said, ". . . like the young sapling, ever growing with the upward thrust of life."

For months I told my pediatrician that something wasn't right about Ned, but he kept saying I was too anxious, to calm down. So I had to play the neurotic mother until, finally, he referred us to Children's Hospital. That's when they found that he has this gland disorder. It's been one long fight to get people to listen, to get some kind of service. And everyone thinking I'm the most aggressive thing that ever came down the pike. But I see him getting worse and worse, and I'll fight this thing—and I'll fight them until they start treating me like I'm not a moron—and giving us some attention. But, for sure, some days I just want to toss in the towel. I'm ready to give up. I lose all faith in everything, and I even begin to wonder about myself. Then we manage a little victory and I know somebody up there likes me, and I go on.

Perhaps it could be said that we need faith in *ourselves* at least as much as we need faith in a society, or humankind, or a higher being. We have the inherent ability to recognize that our knowledge of others and our relationships with them, of each thing that happens in our lives—this knowledge through our senses and in our nature—has rhyme and reason, is beautiful, has love and hope to it as real as dawn; that we, in our most creative moments, consciously sense this orderliness and beauty and love which bespeaks the seamless web of the universe.

We are, at the same time, aware of the limits of the human mind or body, no matter how well it often performs. What haunts us is that this life, which we are ever trying to comprehend, is often strange—often stranger than we know, perhaps even stranger than we can ever know. Mrs. Dennis was tired of life, tired of her husband—a merchant seaman seldom at home—tired of taking care of her six-year-old daughter—an only child who was mentally retarded with cerebral palsy. She insisted that she was going to place her daughter in a residential institution located in a distant state, one which we recognized as disreputable, poorly run, and very expensive. A number of us tried to convey our evaluation of the institution to her, and to help her to see that the daughter's

impairment was not serious enough to warrant institutionalization, that the local community agencies could continue to provide appropriate services. Within six months, however, Mrs.
Dennis had made two visits to the institution, borrowed
thousands of dollars to defray initial expenses, placed her
daughter there, and moved from her residence, initiating a
different style of life for herself. On her final visit with us, she
declared:

**My daughter is never going to be anything but a headache to me
or anyone else. She has no future. And I don't plan to spend the
rest of my life being a slave, twenty-four hours a day taking care
of her and all alone at that—I get no help from him—he goes
around the world not knowing we exist. Well, now it's time for
me to get something out of life. I'm going to start to live again—
for myself.**

Some would frown at this mother's behavior. Others might
conclude that what she did was all she was capable of doing. A
few might declare that, for better or for worse, she simply acted
in accordance with strong personal needs, perhaps in im-
maturity, perhaps during a temporary loss of faith in herself or
the world. It is not easy to know, and sometimes too easy to
condemn.

Many handicapping conditions looked upon only as
"problems" become more complex when they acquire the
characteristic of an "expectancy disorder," that is, when much
of the impairment is related to negative expectations concerning how the child might do or to how others may react to him.
What we expect from a person or situation is determined
primarily by the particular way in which we view that person or
circumstance. And the way we see a thing is affected, for
better or worse, by our own motives or needs. We attend
selectively, reacting to things that confirm and justify expectations, neglecting whatever is contradictory to them.

When we imagine life, we then go on to live what we imagine. No fact exists except as interpreted. If we are optimistic, what follows tends to occur more in favor of what is anticipated. As William James long ago observed, believing that life is worth living will create different facts. Fearful expectations can lead to justifications for one's beliefs. From time to time, a parent *or* child will appear to have a weakening capacity to live life in the present; they live in a state of negative expectancy of "what might be," the fearful expectation of failure or rejection sweetened only by the hope of happier tomorrows. Under such circumstances, the capacity to be oneself fully and spontaneously in the immediate present is reduced. For some, even apparently obvious success cannot be truly enjoyed at the moment it occurs, because there is always the darkened look ahead.

In such ways is the weakening or lack of faith revealed. It may be difficult to regain a firm footing of positive expectancies, to come to believe, as Buber suggested, that every person born into this world represents something new, something that never existed before, something original and unique; to believe that there has never been anyone like you or me or any handicapped child in the world—for if there had been one, there would be no need for the other; to believe that every single one of us is a new thing in the world and is required to fulfill his or her particular function or task.

Some parents seem to have faith which is a particular vision of the world and which leads to creative transformations; they live as though to say, "Whatever good or bad may come to us, we can work to give it meaning, shape it to something of value." Poet John Berry, in his lovely book, *Flight of White Crows*, regards every experience as grand and mystifying, deserving of the respect we might give someone or something we most highly revere.

Faith's way helps us to see beyond the problem, beyond the often trivial, boring, and frustrating to the potentials of ability and goodness held down or hidden underneath. One mother of a retarded child, a very active spokesperson for the rights of handicapped persons, spoke in one of my classes recently and included these thoughts in her presentation:

Speaking for many parents, many of us say, "My faith keeps me going." That doesn't mean that we sit around praying or wishing for a cure or miracle. No, it means that we have the situation pretty well in hand, that our children have reasonably appropriate professional people and friends interested in the child and the family's welfare. Most of us have faith in the future, but we live pretty much one day at a time, and most of us, I believe, get to the point where we are at peace with ourselves. We try not to fool ourselves, but we keep looking for what is possible. We're opportunists.

Let us close this portion with some words from author Pearl S. Buck, who, as the articulate and compassionate mother of a retarded daughter, has inspired countless parents. Once, when asked what her basic beliefs were, she responded:

I believe in human beings but my faith is without sentimentality. I know that in environments of uncertainty, fear . . . the human being is dwarfed and shaped without his being aware of it, just as the plant struggling under a stone does not know its own condition. Only when the stone is removed can it spring up freely into the light. But the power to spring up is inherent. . . .*

*From Pearl S. Buck, "Roll Away the Stone," in *This I Believe,* ed. Edward R. Murrow (New York: Simon & Schuster, 1952), pp. 21–22. Reprinted by permission.

6 BECOMING

I go into a perilous place. There
is but one danger—that I
shall not be myself. Not
that I may pretend, but that
I may not recognize that I am
myself, absolutely imperiled
and absolutely secure.

John Berry (Flight of White Crows
(New York: Macmillan Co., 1961), p. 188.
Reprinted by permission.)

Life, of course, is not always what it seems. Things are not always what they seem. In fact, things may be precisely the opposite of what they seem. As each one of us from time to time recognizes, we ourselves are not always what we may seem. Like T. S. Eliot's Prufrock, we prepare a face to meet the faces we may meet. We try to make an appearance to win approval or the dependence of another person. Rather than being our genuine selves, we cut a figure that becomes an illusion, and we come to treat these phantoms as real. Most of us, I believe, want only to live in agreement with the promptings that flow from our true selves. But why is that so difficult? Consider one mother of a retarded daughter:

Always I've tried to live a good life. I went to church regularly and I thought I was living like a good Christian. But now I see that I was fooling myself. You know, I was the good wife, the good mother, the good neighbor. It comes as a jolt to me to realize that part of me has been acting that way just to make a good impression, to be able to get praise, be able to say to myself, "You're something special." When Bill told me out of a clear sky he couldn't take me and my perfect ways any longer, I was shocked—and very angry too. I couldn't dream he'd do such a thing. I thought it must be something the matter with him—that he had the problem. But slowly I've come to think the cause was the way I lived my life—cleaning all the time, and everything on a schedule, and all the time and worry with the children. So I think now I drove him away—drove him out of the bed, out of the house, out of my life. How simple and silly I was, and how I misjudged myself. It's sad. All that time together and I didn't ever say anything really meaningful.

We are more fully human when we do not seek perfection. Some of us have become aware that we are occasionally willing to commit minor sins in the name of loyalty. Such people do not aspire to sainthood, and many suspect that some who do so aspire have forgotten all that is required to be fully human.

There are parents who bend over backward trying to do the best thing, be the best model for their children, but who too often suppress their own wishes or feelings. It is possible to treat special children *too* specially, to think they must be treated in many ways with kid gloves because in some ways they are different. Sometimes this takes the form of excusing their errors, letting them get away with things ordinarily not allowed, or being overprotective of their feelings. However, a lack of forthrightness with a child often reflects an avoidance of expressing our own true feelings.

One father had been worried for months that his blind son, a high-school student, might not have the academic ability to meet college entrance requirements. He did not know that his son was just as worried. One evening the father, in a moment of frustration, blurted out that he was not sure the son had the stuff to make it, that it was hard enough for those with sight. It was as if a door had opened for, after a long silence, the son spoke: "Dad, I was feeling down and a little worried myself; now, to see that you're feeling the same as I do—well, that's really O.K. And I don't feel quite as alone now. I'd like to talk with you about it."

To level with another is to "ring true" when expressing thoughts or feelings—especially feelings. Leveling in the healthiest sense (which means taking into account our best judgment as to the other person's feelings and ability to cope with honest declarations) is the avoidance of sham or putting up a false front—faking. Leveling clears the air, clarifies feelings through sharing, lets the other know where one stands, and leads to negotiation and helpful intimacy. Parents, as parents or as lovers, cannot always be calm, understanding, patient, and all-knowing—as parents or as lovers.

To level with others, however, requires that we first level with ourselves. We cannot appreciate in another what we have not learned to appreciate in ourselves. Sometimes we are ignorant of ourselves because knowledge of self is painful—we prefer the pleasures of illusion. We want only to be carefree and happy, but to feel true joy or to love fully is possible only if we are also free to risk feeling pain and deep despair. The mother of handicapped twins wrote illuminatingly in her diary:

I sometimes think of myself, not as a person with her own feelings and hopes, but as a robot: "the care-taker." Supplying services as mother or wife everybody takes for granted—except me. I've become separated from the personal me, the real me. It has taken all this time, now that the boys are adolescents, to get back to the real me. I now realize—with some sadness and I'll admit a sense of loss—what I could have been and haven't been—that I've been pulled away from my real self. I was no longer the maker of my behavior. The needs of others shaped my actions—and those actions became my masters. Now I must respond to my own needs, shape my own behavior again after all these years. I want to be the creator of my own behavior, be master—or mistress—of my own fate. I, too, have a life to live! But still, deep inside me, a voice—the old voice I listened to for years—comes back to haunt me, and twinges of guilt and duty and rightness crop up within me. I have to battle these feelings. I wonder if these feelings and all the hopes I have, my own personal longings, I wonder if they make me an unnatural parent.

This parent went on to earn a graduate degree in special education and is working very successfully as a teacher of high-school students with learning disabilites.

The refusal to recognize what to others seems obvious is one of many variations of ways to fool ourselves. Parents of special children sometimes erect defensive armors—denying fact, denying true feeling. As understandable as this may be psychologically, and as much as we may respect their need to behave that way, defensive behavior is antagonistic to the process of personal becoming—it blocks off growth or change for the good. A clinical note from my case history files is illustrative:

Clinical note: Gary's parents were angry today. Complaining about his being picked on again by the neighborhood children. Said that the other parents were keeping their kids away from Gary. Parents seem to blame every problem on his brain injury or hyperactivity. They are not yet able to see that Gary's problems are not simply a matter of hyperactivity, which causes the social rejection. Parents have gone overboard in giving him freedom, perhaps as an overcompensation for guilt feelings. Gary's received apparently very little structure or discipline in his upbringing. He is now a human cyclone, incapable of accepting the rules of any game or social structure. Now he just interrupts others, provokes their anger or rejection. Parents bring up one feeble excuse after another to rationalize his deviant activity, focusing on the congenital brain damage. . . . If any one of this family's lives is to be better, Gary's parents first must change. They need assistance in learning to consider the neighbors' feelings, trying to see things from others' perspective, inaugurating a gradual increase in orderliness in their interactions and attitudes with Gary, achieving greater insight into their own needs and behaviors; they need to receive parent training in changing their behaviors. All of this will require their being honest about Gary, his relationship with others, and, most of all, being open about the impact of their own needs and perspectives on the total situation.

Not surprisingly, the degree to which parents level with others or their children correlates with the degree of leveling characteristic of their own relationship. We disclose ourselves, allow ourselves to become known, to the degree that we believe the other will receive us in good will. I will speak without deception when I sense an attitude of love and trust. To love another is to attempt to know that person better and better, for then one can be more effective in terms of the other's happiness. But one also loves through revealing oneself to the other. This can turn out to be a very frightening thing; while you may share greater love when you reveal yourself, you may also expose yourself to terrible hurt. Once again, then, we encounter the dilemma: (1) to deny the expression of my true self because I may be hurt, or (2) to be myself frankly, openly, and thereby take the risk of pain that accompanies full self-disclosure. Only through authentic *being* can we *become* something more than we are. Our armor may protect us from the misinterpretation or crassness of some others, but we must beware that it doesn't also block out another's tenderness or our own.

Mary, who had been born without ears, once asked her mother, "Did Daddy ever cry?" "Yes," her mother had replied; then, more hesitantly, she continued, "When you were born." "Why did he?" Mary had asked. "Because of his love for you—and for me, too, I think," was the reply. "And perhaps because he thought life for you might be more difficult than usual," her mother went on. "But we've done pretty well, haven't we?" "Yes," Mary answered, "but I think it was nice that Daddy cried for me."

In a discussion group of brothers and sisters of handicapped children, Jim, the older brother of a young boy with cerebral palsy, made the following comment:

The first time I ever saw my father cry was once when he was tired and irritable. He always worked so hard and his mood

usually was fine. But this time Joey was raising cain and spilling food at the table, and my father pushed him back in his seat a little roughly, and he accidentally knocked Joey's glasses off. They broke—they were expensive, special ones. My father just went off into the den, and I saw him crying. I guess I realized then that fathers could cry, too. I think I understood, and it was O.K.

The brilliant father of a severely retarded and malformed infant admitted that he hoped his son would die soon. "We will do everything we can, and we need to know he is well cared for, but the truth is I hope he will die." This was the second child so afflicted within this family. Through several discussions with medical representatives of the hospital, the father realized that the knowledge being gained through study of his child might someday be of value in service to others. He was clearly relieved to be able to think that his child might someday be the source of help to another. "It helps," he stated, "to know that there is *some meaning* possible in all of this."

The grandfather of one of the children in our clinic once spent the morning with us observing the children, chatting with us. "You know," he mused, "These children have no subterfuge; they are all innocence in the direct way they let themselves just act naturally. What they feel, they express. The fakery we develop as adults has not been drummed into them. It is a marvelously human thing."

I knew what he meant. Sometimes all we can do is stand in admiration of human beings, of being human. I recollect the day one of our retarded boys was being tormented by an older group of boys as he left our clinic building. He kept walking, stepped up into his bus, then looked toward them and, in his friendly fashion, smiled. The boys, chagrined, left. Psychiatrist Robert Coles has observed that there could be many scholarly explanations of such a smile. It could have been called a reaction formation, a relfex, a conditioned response to fear, a manifestation of a primitive cortical mechanism. Is it not sufficient to view that smile simply as a moment of blessed graciousness? Of what avail is any scientific explanation—or any attempt at all to interpret? He smiled, they left, his bus pulled away. He has his problems, so do they, so do we all. His was a moment of grace, vital to him—and perhaps to the others. Need more be said?

"Sometimes I think I've chosen the hard way—the way of being honest—but I believe it's the better way in the long run," said the mother of a nine-year-old child with leukemia. She described her attempts to provide a normal environment for her son: "Hospital settings make this difficult." She mentioned the regressions that she now expected, and her son's fright, anger, thumb-sucking, and depression coming and going—depending on changes in his physical condition:

Now, there are no denials, no coverups between us. Now I think there is trust and confidence. He knows what's going on in his own good way; he can tell from the changes in routine, the visits to the different clinics, and so on. But now he knows that he can ask any question and he'll get a straight answer. Oh, we're brief and to the point, and we put it on his level, like "this drug's not working too well right now." The simple answers are the best. Yes, he's asked that question all of the parents in there fear: "Will I die?" We've replied as well as we could. We say that all of us will die. We're not sure exactly when—no one knows that. We're not sure we can always live as long as we'd like to. That's realistic, but it's hopeful, too. Of course, it can't be right for everybody. Each case is a little different. But not telling it like it is—well, we've seen people who do this—and it only makes things more difficult—for the whole family.

Being an authentic human being is perhaps life's most difficult task. Strangely enough, it runs counter to all or most of what we have been taught. Mrs. Baker, who was a veteran of our clinic conference groups with parents, now functioned—as is not infrequently the case with healthy, evolving individuals—as a quasi-counselor during our discussions. At this particular point, she had fixed her helping sights on a young mother of a minimally verbal and maximally aggressive six-year-old boy. This quiet, soft-spoken mother had not once, during six months of weekly discussions, ever voiced unhappiness concerning her relationship with her son. I am certain Mrs. Baker had "diagnosed" a case of denial, defensiveness, and a lack of recognition of her own true feelings in this young mother, who, indeed, always acted so as to "give a good impression." For several weeks, Mrs. Baker had been steadily ruffling her, claiming that nobody could be the angel this mother tried to create the impression of being. Finally, one morning Mrs. Baker asked, "Don't you even ever get just plain bored?" And the young mother opened up, declaring, "His constant repeating over and over again of things he does can drive me crazy. Some days I want to open the window and shout down the street at the top of my lungs, 'Does *anyone* want to have an intelligent conversation?' Then he seems to sense this and goes for my jugular all the more." At least, however, with this breakthrough of honest feeling, movement from appearance to genuineness had begun. Mrs. Baker, incidentally, although she laughed at pretension and foolish pride, never failed, at the same time, to respect the humanity of the pretender.

No discussion dealing with "seeming" and "being"—much less "becoming"—in relation to handicapping conditions should neglect those processes as they apply to professional workers in their daily rounds with impaired children and their families. I constantly ask myself questions: Is my therapy autobiographical or is it fictional? Am I ringing true or am I role-playing merely for the sake of appearance? Do I do, especially in terms of the desires of others, what I think I *ought* to do, or what I deeply feel and believe I *want* to do?

It is remarkable how much better parents can feel when they realize that the counselor (to whom in their own need they had perhaps already attributed characteristics of perfection) is at least something like them—a person who, for example, knows what it is to have problems. As one father commented, "When you said you were ready to give up on me, I felt for the first time that we had something in common. Before, I just couldn't get on your wavelength, or at least I didn't think you could ever get on mine." It is remarkable how frequently counselors, although they might not wish to be thus characterized, present to their clients the image of an apparently flawless person. Counselor authenticity means that the feelings one is experiencing are not only consciously available, but that one is able to live those feelings, and to share them when appropriate. Some believe the therapy relationship unreal if, over a long period of time, the counselor never expresses annoyance, skepticism, or similar feelings. There are limits to such expressions of authenticity, but to be rigidly consistent or to try to present a perfect image (which is impossible for others to match) eventually erodes the relationship.

An astute mother of a multiply handicapped adolescent once said to me, "I realize that, despite years of working with handicapped persons, professional workers must feel some anxiety in the presence of these severe disorders, if not as suggestive of what their own children's lives might be, then at least as a reminder of their own frailty or mortality. Such experiences are too close and real to be completely unaffecting—or denied." Another mother, speaking to a class of students of child psychiatry, was asked what physicians can do when they are not sure of themselves and don't want to worry the parents. "Just be honest with us," was her reply.

A physician friend of mine, a general practitioner, once confided in me:

Look, most of us know precious little about these severe childhood disorders. If we hold off the diagnosis, in order to be sure so as not to cause unnecessary worry, one out of five of them will curse us later for not telling them sooner. If we refer for a second diagnosis, we can be accused of avoiding a realistic confrontation. Yet it is wise policy to verify your own evaluations in these critical circumstances. Then, if we are too upbeat about the child's chances for happiness or his capability, maybe we set their hopes too high, and perhaps they're later hurt all the more. Oh, I can be honest all right, but how can I be sure they can handle what I might honestly say? So sometimes I hold back a little, out of respect for their feelings.

One parent felt grateful to "the doctors who had been callous" in their treatment. "If they had been kind," she added, "I never would have fought so hard to prove them wrong." She reminded me of the old axiom that one cannot build except on a resisting foundation.

In a trusting, authentic relationship, the mood to risk is one each of us sometimes must take if we are to unmask ourselves and work toward individual human authenticity. To be authentic is to invent oneself—to become something more than one is; the epitome of self-invention is to create oneself in a helping relationship with another—in mutual creativity or becoming. The authentic, fully being, fully becoming person might conclude this section by these few additional remarks:

I do not *need to prove*—how much I do for my child; how much I care, how much I love. I do not pretend to be what I am not; I am fully myself—therefore, I do not mind that others see me as I am. I push aside the impossible burden of always trying to be as strong and well-adjusted as I think others would hope me to be, as available as those who have need of me want me to be. I must learn increasingly to honor the privilege of simply getting tired, becoming a little silly, of accepting the help that those who have need to help me offer. To adjust to this world means that I have to reject much of myself because there are dangerous, forbidden elements. But these very inner recesses also hold vast resources, the wellsprings of my spontaneous behaviors, my joys, my playfulness, my love, my passion, and my creative impulses. If I deny my hellish impulses, might I not also deny my heavenly ones? I will not deny what I am, but I believe that creative effort can serve to harness and unify conflicting elements. In a sense, all of my life is a search and a struggle for socially and personally productive self-consistency, self-creativity, authentic being, and becoming, wholeness, unity.

If the sun and the moon should doubt,
They'd immediately go out.

William Blake, Auguries of Innocence

DOUBTING

In the face of impairment, it is sometimes difficult to believe that we are greater than our faults or our heartaches. There is grief, anguish, shock, disbelief. A part of one has been cut off, perhaps maimed or lost forever. And the depth of the wound is invisible to most if not all others. Here is the clear reminder, we feel, that life's dreams cannot always reach fruition. Here is the fact that separates us from typical, everyday reality, causes us to rage at the apparently smooth ongoing flow of others in the world. Yet even our shouts of rage do not begin to fill the emptiness.

He sits on the floor and twirls—pushes himself around like his legs were the hands of a clock. And like a clock he practically never stops turning. Yet he never speaks, never listens, never looks at you, never answers—just spins all day long, day after day, like a machine. But a machine breaks down once in a while—or you can turn it off. But how do I turn him off, get him to do other things, become something more than, well, a clock, a machine?

It takes a while to realize that deep and prolonged sorrow or even despair are usually not simply the signs of weakness or neurosis. Sorrow is a humanly natural and understandable reaction to a cruel fact, a radically altered reality. And while parents of nonimpaired children have to weather many a storm with their children, most can anticipate their children's continuing development toward eventual maturity and self-sufficiency. The parents of a seriously impaired child may have far less to look forward to. The doubts and despair will often continue in some way for the rest of their lives, including a perhaps woeful expectation of what will happen after the parents have died. The older sister of one severely retarded adolescent reflected these sadder feelings but placed them in a larger perspective:

Yes, a mood of sadness often comes to our house. I have never known it to be absent and I think it will always be with us, like an occasional rainstorm, you might say. Yet between those dark clouds, we've always been able to appreciate his little achievements and to really enjoy many times together. Some think my parents bear a burden—and, in a way, it is a special burden. But I see my parents as having stood up to an awful lot with courage over the years. Still, there really have been moments of happiness, of good fun.

The mother of two retarded children, in a moment of despair coupled with some frustration and anger, said:

Here I am, a poor creature with feelings who *thinks,* who has hungers and conflicts and confusions, who wants so much to love and be loved, and silly people expect me all the time to do all the right things, as though they were saying, "All right, now, be God-like!"

A member of a group of parents of stuttering adolescents spoke sadly of her son's hunger to speak fluently, his feelings of insecurity and doubt. She shared with the group part of a note written by her son:

Can I speak when I need to? I never know. I'm never sure. I'm never able to count on saying one word. Never, never. And then I try again. Whose fault is it? Is it my fault? Was it all in the cards? Have I given myself this out—my speech? But I have a perfectly good mind. Strangely enough, it's my mind that's killing me. It picks on every failure. It compares me with people who can do for themselves. It tortures me. Why can't I use it to solve my problems?

It is not always possible to agree with Shakespeare: "Sweet are the uses of adversity." But certainly, out of despair may arise courage, new ways of coping with life's challenges, faith in the future and hopefulness enough. A boy of fourteen, obese, a severe stutterer with a pock-marked face said to me, after being laughed at for the hundredth time, "Why am I so depressed? They *laughed* at me again. How can I relate my condition to humor? One pratfall may be laughable, but when it's repeated over and over again you lose your taste for it. In the dungeon even the hyena is quiet." He was on the verge of suicide. He went on, however, and at seventeen he said, "Life has meaning if and when one possesses either the comforts of a memorable past, a present filled with joy in its half-shell—that is, peace of mind—or a future with some promise or hope. I have not had that past, I do not have that present, but now I have a future with some hope." And at nineteen he wrote, "Somehow a shaft of light broke through. Possibly it was the attentiveness of some people toward me, or seeing a little girl picking leaves off a tree and putting them to her lips, or the smell of black maple under an autumn sky."

The wellspring of hope may arise and the pall of despair may dissipate anywhere at any time. What is needed is an attitude of readiness to what may be possible. Every life may be remarkable. May we respect every life as though it were something wondrous if not yet fully realized or understood!

Unquestionably, all children doubt themselves, and so do all parents. Especially might they doubt—quite naturally from time to time—their ability to raise their impaired children well. Most parents realize that they cannot, in any broad sense, rely on anyone other than themselves to care for their offspring. Most rely on their own judgment. But most need and deserve professional support in feeling competent to make decisions affecting their children's—and their own—welfare. Most need to know that professional workers have confidence that parents ultimately will make good decisions, given reasonable circumstances. Most parents will welcome professionals who will explore with them possibilities for meeting their problems, who will support them in adjusting to decisions made, and who will act as sounding boards against which to test their own thinking.

All parents make mistakes in bringing up children, but they should not be made to feel guilty about them. I remember a parent saying to her counselor, "I've made some mistakes with Larry, but you have never put me on the defensive about them." "How could I?" he replied. "Perhaps if I had been in your situation, I might have done exactly the same thing."

When I was a very young man, just beginning clinical work, a wise mother one morning took me aside after a parent group meeting and said, "I'm going to tell you a little secret, and someday maybe you'll tell me if I'm wrong. It's this: What looks to you professional people like feelings of guilt or some neurotic sorrow we parents have is very often just our earnest concern with our child's welfare mixed with grief over his handicap." In the years since then, many other parents have made similar helpful contributions to my education. To my mind comes the lively image of Mrs. Muir, mother of two retarded daughters and grandmother of two retarded children, pointing her finger at a group of professional workers at a symposium and speaking intently:

We are people. Need more than that be said? But we are people with a special sorrow. We have our weaknesses and our strengths, like every other parent. But we also have this special sorrow, and it sometimes magnifies life's usual problems, and sometimes you get the repercussions of that. But we are not in the general sense neurotic or abnormal personalities. You cannot generalize about us anymore than you should generalize about children, even—and perhaps especially—retarded children.

A father whose only child died of leukemia and who had become sorely depressed wrote a letter to me recently, a portion of which follows:

At the beginning we asked the usual questions—might it be anything in the diet; could we have done something about it; or, could we have discovered it earlier—questions like that. It just never dawns on you that it could be anything so serious. She had missed some school, had some ear and throat infections. Then one day she had a seizure after a shot of penicillin. Then her lackadaisical behavior, the steady fatigue, and high fevers. And through it all the not really knowing, the not wanting to know, the feelings of helplessness. I could feel myself going downhill with her. I spent a lot of time with her. My wife couldn't take it, couldn't really. Then the doctors spoke in terms of remission rather than cure. What else could they do, I suppose. These stages of her illness keep coming back to me, like signposts on a highway to oblivion. The drugs, which increased her appetite. Then, later, the radiation therapy, and that drug—Vincristine, was it—that caused her hair to fall out. My God, like so many parents, I guess I thought the treatment seemed more horrible than the disease. And then she was gone. And for a while, I was gone—really wiped out. For about a year there. . . . One day I realized that the heartache had turned to boredom. I said to myself, "If you're bored, you're probably boring to be with." And it was true. If you're interested, people will find you interesting. And if you like yourself, people will like you. And if you're happy, people you come in touch with will be. . . . In my sorrow, I had let myself become a dry desert, dull, deadly, repetitious, and empty. So I began going out, meeting and being with people again, and I seem to be doing well. . . . Every so often I look back over my shoulder and realize that the whole experience taught me much. You have to go beyond certainty—there is no such thing—no absolute guarantees. Everything—we ourselves, others—everything is in the final analysis a mystery—at least the answers to the important human conditions. There are just some things we cannot ever know. But I do not despair in this realization— somehow, it rather has served in some crazy sense to increase my awareness of all that is—*now*. . . . I now accept and relish that. Yes, the land under our feet is ours only on loan. . . .

For some parents, the negative feelings persist. Guilt sometimes persists, reminding me of John Masefield's lines in his poem "The Seekers": "Not for us are content, and quiet, and peace of mind. For we go seeking a city that we shall never find."*

In recollecting parents who seemed particularly burdened by guilt, I think of statements made by several:

Like any worker, I am personally responsible for what I make.

At times I sense in my depths that there are no limits to my weaknesses, my depressions and self-doubts.

I pick and pry at myself in perpetual self-analysis, thereby only increasing my self-consciousness and my torment.

I feel responsible for this child *forever*; my other children will grow and leave on their own. This child will always be my burden.

For most of us, sorrow, fear, or doubt can be overcome mainly by way of a cause greater than our own self-interests. It

*From *Poems by John Masefield* (New York: Macmillan Co., 1955), p. 50.

may be the welfare of a child, a spouse, or a larger group of persons in need. Some of us are able to decrease doubts not by searching for what life actually means, but by seeking meanings it *may* have for *us*. The difference is one of feeling imprisoned by present circumstances compared to one of imagining the possibilities. I once asked a group of parents of variously impaired children to bring in several lines or a full poem that might reflect one of their dominant moods. One parent brought in this couplet by William Blake:

A fathomless and boundless deep,
There we wander, there we weep.

Such materials led to helpful discussions in which the group concluded that the individual condition of each of us is tragic, that each of us in any final analysis is alone, but that from time to time, through love or other creative relationship, we escape from the sorrowful solitary state. They also concluded that despair and doubt devitalize, interfere with sound thinking, sap energy, and, finally, isolate. Later, they would go on to the additional conclusion that it is so much more *interesting* and *agreeable* to be an outgoing, mindful, and alive person.

Speaking of doubt brings to mind a pleasant association: I once asked a very wise mother who had been doing some part-time work in our clinic *why* she seemed so successful in her work with the clinic children, although she had no professional training. She replied, "When I'm in doubt, I just try to do what is kind and important. If I'm *really* in doubt, I try to give them what I myself need." Being an emotionally healthy person, she was quite successful with this idea: *Give what you yourself need.*

However, other parents have not progressed to such a happy state. They still speak with disbelief, resentment, or chronic sorrow. They see their plans for the future thwarted, their previous sacrifices meaningless. Others experience a mixture of feelings, which they may regard as unnatural: As the mother of a recently deceased child said, "I still feel guilt but I feel relief now, and regrets, too. I haven't sorted everything out yet." The year before, this mother, in a discussion in our clinic, expressed what to many are inadmissible thoughts:

Sometimes I have death wishes about Tommy. Oh, they're fantasies that slip in and out of my mind—accidents of different kinds. Other times I go to the opposite extreme and I'm unbelievably overconcerned about his health and safety. I can talk about it now that I know I'm not the only one who has these thoughts. Before, I thought I was an evil person. Now I don't think I am. I think a lot of people in my situation would act as I do. Most would not admit it, or could not, and there is a kind of loss in that.

Several years ago one of our evening groups got into several months of weekly discussion based on this premise: It is helpful for people to confront dying—our own or our children's—before we can successfully encounter living. The group became more aware that there are many "little deaths" that occur in a lifetime, and these can serve to help us to reduce the fear of dying. Asked to cite examples of *le petit morte,* they mentioned these: prolonged periods of enforced silence; being very ill; having a bad accident or close call; being separated from a close friend, relative, or lover; being unrequited in love; being depressed; being in an endlessly boring situation; being hurt deeply or surprisingly by someone you care for; seeing your child hurt or in pain; deep disappointment in your child's behavior, your spouse's, your own. The major conclusion this group reached was that the more varied and full their lives were, and the more they were able to be creative in their behavior or relationships, the better equipped they would be to manage death-related events.

For many parents, it is doubt that gnaws. But there is also

the courage of one's doubts—the doing *without* being certain whether one is doing the best thing. He who runs *no* risk takes a *tremendous* risk. Perhaps, as the poet John Berry once suggested, if we knew *all* the facts, we should never dare move even one little finger of our own accord. Perhaps! The young father of a severely handicapped son, whose wife had died during the child's birth, related the following to me recently:

Sometimes I see myself as the White Knight in search of the Holy Grail. What do I search for? Fulfillment for my son—for my own ability to do the wisest thing. The goal is distant, and I'm not sure of the way or the dangers that lie ahead. People help. Everyone's rooting for me. But deep inside I fear I may fail no matter how hard I may try. Getting the pot of gold at the end of the rainbow may not be possible.

Other times, I'm something out of the theatre of the absurd. I have a goal, but it seems there's no way to reach it. Some people help, more serve as obstructions—all the rules and the lack of public understanding. Most are indifferent. Sometimes it seems nobody really knows just what to do. Then I feel doomed. Still I pursue relentlessly, work as hard as I can, do all I can, wanting my son to be all that he deserves to be. Often I'm struck by the crazy things that happen to us. Sometimes, for a minute, I even wonder if I'm out of contact, if it's all a dream. But it's not a dream. It's not necessarily a nightmare, but it isn't a dream.

Each morning of each day, each of us tries to find answers to life's elementary questions, most of which seem to relate to what meaning or value is to be attributed to our lives. We frequently encounter mystery. Each time we are reminded of the limits of the mind. The explanation that is full and satisfying is not forthcoming. To the mind eager for certainties, such ruminations must be humbling. And yet it is precisely at the point of humility that perhaps the grasping of anything about the essence of life is possible.

The reasons for my depressions I know. They have become far less interesting to me than my efforts to cope. I've kept going on faith. Now I discover that, quite often, the performance of everyday chores cracks that dreary wall. Feeding the dogs, cat, and birds; watering the plants. As I do these simple things, my spirits rise.

When I'm tense or anxious, I simply think of someone I love very much, and this produces an immediate calming effect, a sense of peace and happiness—if I can will myself to think of them in the first place.

I recently saw a mother who, several months ago, seemed quite despondent. Now she looked alive and happy. I asked her what accounted for the difference. She replied, "During one of our discussions we mentioned that life could be satisfying if one had something to work for, something to love, and something to hope for. I realized that I really had all three and must keep all those ways alive." We spoke of her son, a lad of extremely limited ability, of the family's struggles to pull all its resources together for the greater welfare of all members, of the sometimes painful anticipation of what the future might bring. "The changes in my son are often heartbreakingly small," she continued, "but there's no doubt that our lives have been enriched in some measure." This mother, herself often in pain from a chronic arthritic condition, was an inspiration to all who knew her. "I have learned," she once said, "that there are eternal things that I can count on, not simply the endless minutiae that crowd our way. There is love that lasts, and beauty that endures." As someone has said, "The rose will wither, and some day die, but it is no less worth tending and growing."

8 TRUSTING

Keep alive the dream. As long
as you have a dream in your
heart, you cannot lose the
significance of living.

Dean Howard Thurman, in a speech at Boston University

One of the members of our parent group, frustrated and angry, declared, "In God we trust! Well, I trusted in God and he betrayed my trust—at least that's what I thought at first. Then I calmed down and got to thinking about it more clearly. I realized that if my home, my life were to go to pieces, then surely it must be a house of cards. I decided then that it wasn't a house of cards, and it wouldn't fall apart. I suppose you could say I regained my trust—in God or the future, or maybe in myself." This commentary occurred during a discussion of "trust." We found it very difficult to pin down in concrete terms, yet the consensus was that trust is important, even critical, in successful coping as parents of impaired children. What is trust? The following responses were among those offered:

Trust is when you put your faith in somebody—you believe in them.

To trust another person means that you can count on her to act with your best interests in mind.

Trust is when I can put myself in their hands.

I can trust somebody if I can say anything to them and they can accept it.

You can be natural, be yourself, go with the flow, and it's O.K. with the one you can trust.

If I can trust somebody, then I don't have to be afraid, I can relax. I can just say, "That's fine." He would be like a kind father.

Clearly, trust is related to faith. Trusting another is to relinquish, to let go. It includes an element of risk, perhaps a leap into the unknown. Trust requires courage. In exceptionality, it may include a belief by the counselor in the parent, or by the parent in the child, or in their ability to grow together in their own way. It includes trusting the other, while making mistakes, and also to learn from those mistakes. Trust embraces belief in the capability of the person to develop the human potential that exists within. Such trust is not easily faked; it is not simply a technique. One can only be as trusting as one actually is. But if one is as fully and genuinely trusting as capacity allows, the effects will be salutary.

Children are not born with trust; they must develop it. And they develop it primarily through interaction with their parents, as was the case with eighteen-year-old Paul, who had been a hell-raiser when younger:

My father deserted us, but my mother was always there. I could always count on her. She was my oak tree. I would run to her when things got stormy—when the truant officer or the police were after me, stuff like that. She always bent, never broke. I trust her more than anyone in the world.

You have to *test* before you can *trust.* Many a child's worrisome behavior is a testing of parents and others: Will they still love me, will they still like me even when I am difficult to live with? (Perhaps it is simply very important for him really to know.) Even among adults, a surprising confidence shared with us by another may actually be but a test of how trustworthy we are.

Inability to trust others under typical circumstances closes one off from social experiences, while to trust others blindly in all situations may be equally incapacitating—one may become a target for abuse or exploitation. It is not always easy for parents to find counselors in whom they can place full trust. Too many have experienced misunderstanding, rigid diagnostics, or a lack of simple sympathy.

We had gone to nine different places in five years. We got a different answer each and every time—"retarded," the first one said; "aphasic," the second one said; then we got "autistic," "hard of hearing," and "minimally brain-damaged." The best one was "developmental delay." Finally we found Dr. Marholin, and he just said to us, "Let's not call him anything. Let's observe him together for a while, then decide what behaviors we'd like to change—to get rid of or to add. Then we'll work—all of us—you at home and we here in the clinic—to obtain the goals we set." And our son's been progressing ever since. Dr. Marholin was straight with us, he didn't put on professional airs or use a lot of fancy language, and he wasn't all dollars and cents. His interest in our problems was genuine, and he put an awful lot of honest effort into our lives. Yes, I'd put our son in his hands without blinking an eye.

A parent, teacher, or counselor may show a lack of trust in different ways: by trying to squeeze the child into a behavioral mold or even, perhaps, by caring too much or by overprotection. Trust mistrusts indoctrination. Indoctrination serves most to satisfy the needs of the indoctrinator, not the needs of the one to be helped. Faith, trust, and love are the blood and bones of creative counseling, education, or parenthood. And among the basic personal building-blocks, *self-trust* must be one of the most necessary.

The six months following Eddie's bike accident were sheer torture for my husband and me. After he died, I didn't want to get close to another child—I was afraid I'd be badly hurt again. But you can't do that, cut yourself off from life. Maybe it was my brother's children, or seeing the other kids on the playground, or a certain feeling of emptiness, but gradually I got to be busy as hell again, and we made the most of whatever life had to bring. Then Brad was born with cerebral palsy! Funny, I remember one night late alone out in the backyard, and I looked up at the sky and spoke to God: "God," I said, "you pulled a swifty on me. You have some of the devil in you, I think. Why me? Why us?" But by then I loved the little rascal so much, it wasn't a big problem. I guess I've answered myself by staying in there pitching, doing just all I can do and not expecting miracles. But at rock bottom it's trust—a trust in a higher element I somehow, in some strange way, feel more friendly with, but it's more than that. It's more a trusting of myself, and knowing that I greet most days with some joy.

Self-trust respects one's own feelings, helps to separate real from apparent problems, increases the strength to believe in one's own conclusions. Self-trust coexists with willingness to open onself to the immediate present rather than seeking refuge in the concrete "known." Self-trust moves toward letting the future happen rather than trying always to shape it to become a carbon copy of the past. And self-trust puts one in a position to risk much, including the anger or lack of understanding of others.

Frankly, by the time Shirley became physically mature, we were usually fatigued, constantly fighting off exhaustion. Maybe we were just getting older, but I think it was more all those sleepless nights with her prowling around, turning on the stove—things like that, you know. Anyway, with her child's mind and her adult requirements, she'd become even angrier, more frustrating and demanding. She bit, kicked, threw things—and she's strong. Only then, after all those tough years, did we find this community home. Oh, our friends and the professional people couldn't understand why we did it—how could they know what we went through?

But now, there she's happy. If people ask, we don't feel guilty. We know how difficult the decision was—all the moaning and the tears about it and looking at everything from every angle. We know. But we made the decision, we take the responsibility, and we're all happier for it. I shake my head when I think of what our lives might have been if she stayed with us, with her cramping our lives, and we unable to handle her. It's good to know she's in a proper place, getting good help twenty-four hours a day, and with a kind of dignity, you know, a kind of dignity she deserves because she's cared for and she's as independent as it's possible for her to be.

Perhaps it is in the consideration of possible removal from the home or institutionalization that some of the most anguishing and challenging aspects of parenting and counseling occur. And it is at just such a point that trust of another and self-trust are both most critical and most severely tested. This is as true for the counselor as it is for the parent. Indeed, although we know less of this component of trust, it is probably at least as critical a time in terms of the trust of the *child* in the goodwill of those involved in the decision—especially, of course, the parents. The counselor may offer suggestions, but the importance of parental responsibility in such vital decisions is paramount. Only the parents, after thorough appraisal of the entire situation and all of its complex ramifications, can make truly adequate decisions. Talking to parents of other handicapped children is usually helpful. Feelings, alternate solutions, and planning deserve careful working through. Professional counseling may be very useful. Parents may be extremely hostile and defensive or very cooperative, although most function somewhere between these two extremes. It is hardly surprising if a whole gamut of often conflicting emotions and alternative plans are worked through, for the decisions under consideration are momentous ones.

We would, each of us, wish to trust—not foolishly but

mindfully. Our intention would be to remain fully available to the other, with an open mind and heart. Such would be the character of a dialogue with trust. Out of these soils might we then conclude: Life's relationships rise or fall, are beautiful or empty, harming or loving, to the degree that trust is present or absent.

Knowledge of certain sorts cannot
be proved . . . but it (stands)
in no more need of proof than
the beauty of a sunset or
the terrors of the night.

*Carl G. Jung (Memories,
Dreams and Reflections,* ed.
Aniela Jaffe [New York: Vintage
Books, 1961], p. 92)

KNOWING

"Know thyself" reads the maxim atop the temple of Apollo at Delphi. In his *Apology,* Plato has Socrates say, "The un-examined life is not worth living." Perhaps we could say, in one sense, that all of life is a search to find ourselves, a journey of self-discovery. Some of us search frantically to find the elusive "something" that will bring all of the scattered elements of our lives into fruitful harmony. Others relinquish the search, halt the journey—out of despair, perhaps, or possibly even fear of what we may discover. Yet others search for we know not what—or where.

Martin Buber, one of the century's most important rep-resentatives of the human spirit, wrote a valuable little book, *The Way of Man,* a collection of short essays interpreting traditional Hasidic stories. The book very simply but exquisitely examines and explains the basic tenets of a way of life that lies near the center of Judaism. Among his citations are the say-ings of the sages: Know whence you came, whither you are going, and to whom you will have to render accounts. At another point he reminds us that the foremost task of all per-sons is the actualization of their unique and never-recurring potentialities, and not simply the repeating of what another has done. He mentions Rabbi Zuzya who said, a short while before his death, "In the world to come, I shall not be asked, 'Why were you not Moses?' I shall be asked, 'Why were you not Zuzya?' " Why are we not ourselves? *The Way of Man* builds to the conclusion that the treasure each individual seeks cannot, as the ancient story goes, be found anywhere in the world and yet, nevertheless, there is a place where it can be found: It is in the place where one stands, here where one stands. The father of a ten-year-old boy who had recently died of leukemia had obviously learned this:

My relationship with Robbie was not the best. He never confided in me as much as with his mother, maybe saw me as an intrusion in his relationship with her. But one night we went fishing and caught some good ones and talked and—it was the only time he told me he loved me. Robbie knew he was dying. We didn't talk about death much, but when we did we'd be as honest as we could about it. Then our friends started telling us to go to faith healers and things like that. We never did. We're not religious people. And anyway, we finally knew he wasn't going to pull through. And he knew it, too. That day he just said to the Doctor, "No more," meaning he didn't want the needle anymore, and the Doc asked Robbie if he knew what that meant and Robbie said, "Yes, I'm going to die." And the way he handled it—was wonderful. I quit my job to work at home, to be with him—he didn't like the hospital and so we decided he'd be home with us until the end. I did a lot of soul-searching. My son taught me a lot about myself. And my wife was wonderful all the way through. It's one hell of a way to learn about yourself and your relationships, but it is a way.

Sometimes, as Ben Franklin declared, the things that hurt instruct. It is one way to know or to know oneself. There are many ways of knowing or of self-knowing. There is the knowing of the other's needs, the knowing of one's capacity to respond to the other, the knowing of facts, and the deeper knowing of feeling—mind knowledge and blood knowledge.

There is also the knowing that is anxiety-connected. Experienced clinicians become familiar with parents who have a "drive for closure," who need to know exactly what is wrong and precisely what "it" is called, preferably in single terms. Or the parent who offers the clinician two alternatives for consideration: "Is Billy a brain-damaged child or is he not?" "Is he mentally slow or is he not?" "Will he be able to speak within a year's time or not?" Such times are difficult and perhaps threatening for professional workers. If they are themselves insecure, they may become trapped into premature diagnosis and labeling. On the other hand, they may recognize the deeply felt need of the parent to *know,* to resolve the nagging doubt.

At least, I thought I would have the relief of knowing, after for so long not knowing. I wanted so badly to simply know. I'd grab at any straw.

Clinicians may consider it vital to the family's welfare to keep all possible options open, especially in instances of difficult differential diagnosis. They may also consider it important to try to help the parents to increase their ability to live with some doubt but with improved comfort.

I gradually moved away from unfulfillable dreams that could not be fulfilled toward realities that could.

The "need to know" is a pervasive one, and understandably so. A fixed belief, an exact conclusion, or an apparent "fact" may be very comforting, but such apparent certainties may be deceptive, too. So much in life that is important can never be pinned down precisely. The plans we make, the ideals we pursue, the relations we dimly discern that seem to make sense, the joys and sorrows we experience—none of these as such can be neatly weighed on a scale. And yet, without these immaterial qualities, life would be a universe of matter without meaning.

I once asked a group of psychotherapists if it might not be

possible to design a poetic conception of behavior disorders. Most professional conceptions are rational ones—of course, they have value. Is there a place for a poetic image? It would be related, not to merely *describing* and *analyzing* behavior, but to a way of actually *experiencing* it—experiencing what the disordered human experiences—as a way of being or behaving within it, a way of sensing it and relating to it, acting upon it, a way of becoming more deeply receptive to it. This would be a way, I imagine, much like what a loving mother or father experiences in their most deeply sympathetic relationships with their children.

I suspect, also, that it would be that deeply experienced feeling-in-relationship that constitutes the essence of actualized good "motherliness" and "fatherliness," or "brotherliness" and "sisterliness". E. E. Cummings once said that poetry was feeling—not knowing or believing or thinking, expressing nobody but yourself in words. Whenever we think or believe, he suggested, we're a lot of other people, but the moment we simply feel, we're nobody but ourselves. I believe one could profitably apply such thoughts to life with impaired children, as parent or as helping worker. There are different ways of knowing.

Always, however, we return to the basic realization that the greatest challenge in knowing is that related to knowing self. In each life there are critical moments that tell us more about ourselves than all the rest of our lives put together. The moment when we learn that a child is impaired or imperiled in some way may be such a time. Could we say that there is no thought or action that is not in some sense autobiographical? Each expression, if we but comprehend the code, reveals something about ourselves. It is an ancient observation that the things we see are but the things that are in us. What we see or interpret in the behavior of children often is in ourselves, not in the children whose behavior we are interpreting.

The impression my child makes on me changes according to how *I* feel. Sometimes I see the devil in him and other times I see magical things. But I have slowly come to see that the bad or the beautiful, the magic—they're mostly within me.

I was deeply honored by another single parent, one whom I had encouraged to keep a diary, who later shared her writings with me. She kept her diary in the form of a running letter to her son, who had suffered extensive brain-damage in an automobile accident. The moving quality of her statement was, I thought, enormous:

Dear Son:
I am coming to know myself through you. Perhaps you will come to know yourself in important ways through me. Perhaps I can truly experience something of what you experience. I hope I can. I want to be able to see things from your viewpoint. I think, too, that I need to have you see things from my perspective. Perhaps one day you will. Will you know how difficult it is to be a parent? To try to make sense out of the whole, crazy patchwork that is our lives? I can never hope to embrace the whole of it, to see the whole scene laid out clearly before me. But I try to give each life-piece a feeling of the whole, to respect it, to give myself fully to it, try to know its essential thought in the most human way. Will you appreciate my love of beauty? This piece of pottery I lift from the table, this woodcut before me, brings tears to my eyes; they are so beautiful. This lovely mood of bittersweetness I feel so deeply. It is not unlike the mood I sometimes find myself flowing into late at night, as I look at you sleeping. I want you to know these feelings—to know I have them—and perhaps to know them yourself some day. I want you to know me, not just as a provider, but in these other ways, too.

Occasionally, in parent group discussions, we will select a "carrier phrase" as a springboard to discussion. For example: "I care for myself. . . ." All individuals complete the phrase in their own way, with a group discussion following each individual's own completions of the statement. Other helpful carrier phrases we have used include these: "I commit myself to . . . ; I am aware of . . . ; I respect myself because . . . ; I matter to myself because . . . ; I value myself because . . . ." In one session, a divorced mother raising five children, including two with severe learning disabilities, spoke positively:

I respect myself because I've come to realize that not only do I try to do the right things with the children, but I really can't *help* but do the right thing. It's ingrained in me, I guess. But I took your advice and I'm reading Anne Lindbergh's book, *Gift from the Sea*. It's a beautiful book. She says that in order to find your life you must lose it. I'm not sure she means in the sense that I seem to have lost mine—in trying to do for the whole family, working and all, without help.

Another group member responded:

No, she doesn't mean finding yourself that way. She means doing something creative—oh, I know you can be creative with your kids, but outside that—finding yourself in some other activity that's not your everyday thing. Of course, with five children and a full-time job, it's—well, I'm not sure how you'd do it.

A third parent added:

Maybe this group can be your escape. Maybe we can help you to find yourself again. I wouldn't think you'd ever get a chance to think of yourself. Here you can. And you know, there's one other place you can be alone and quiet and gather yourself together, calm down. It's my own particular secret place. My once-a-week hour alone at church. It's been my one guaranteed hour-for-me for years.

Self-evaluation in the best sense is not merely circular rumination but an opening up, a reaching out, a going beyond pure self. True, it can be self-torture; discoveries about oneself are *not* always of the happy kind. But the risk must be taken if self-knowing is to continue—the step into the deep well of basic feeling and true self-confrontation. What am I trying to do? What am I really saying to others? To myself? What am I most sensitive to? What am I most angry about? What are my greatest doubts, comforts, delights, fantasies, fears, hopes? Perhaps we must, as Carl Jung avers, let in the darkness, "the shadow."

Parent and child, husband and wife, friend and friend—we may never know ourselves fully, may never meet fully any more than sunset and dawn will ever meet. But the best approximation to the full awareness and being-in-relationship can make life worthwhile. The task of each of us is to come to know ourselves and one another, to be open and loving, to respect and even to hold the other in reverence.

In the Talmud we read: "If I am not for myself, who will be?" The young mother of a retarded child spoke perhaps as eloquently:

No one knows me the way I know myself. I know my feelings and my potentials. I know I can grow and shape my own future. I've said *yes* to myself!

HOPING

In the dead cold of winter
I ask myself why I live where I
do, and I get my answer
every spring.

Yankee Farmer

83

Mrs. Moser, the mother of an eight-year-old, minimally verbal, emotionally erratic boy had recently been notifed that her son had muscular dystrophy, and now the full realization of the implications of the illness took hold. "It was easy to keep going when I thought the answer was just around the corner. When even one little good prediction about Bobby came true, I felt great." She looked through our clinic one-way viewing mirror at Bobby, in the midst of active children, looking more listless each day. "But lately my confidence is cut off pretty badly. I must admit I'm pretty depressed. My fight has left me. My determination's gone." She looked at me directly, saying, "You know, it's hard to go on when you can't see any way out of your difficulty."

These words of despair could have been spoken by any parent. I think of a woman whose husband had abandoned her and their six children, including cerebral-palsied Linda. I also recall Mrs. M., the unwed, depressed mother of a boy who is now eight years old and severely retarded, and so many others in the grip of melancholy or hopeless desperation. Yet, all but a very few of the thousands of parents I have known have gone beyond their winters of discontent. How? Why? The answers to such questions are never simple. But there appears to be one characteristic common to all who vanquish despair: Hope is *not* abandoned.

But by that hope I mean the imagining of *real* things, the imagining of things that really have the possibility of coming true. I do not mean the hope which is but fantasy and which cannot be worked out in the actual world. I have known a number of parents who have, usually unwittingly, encouraged their impaired children to pursue goals most would judge to be far beyond reach. Jimmy, for example, was a bright and personable lad whose one wish was to be a sports announcer. Jimmy listened month after month to the countless popular music programs on radio and television, and he imagined himself becoming one of the talkmasters whose words livened his days. But as a severely cerebral-palsied, hearing-impaired individual whose speech was barely understandable, and whose prognosis for significant speech improvement was poor, the hope was linked more to fantasy than reality. In the sometimes prolonged "home-boundedness" of cerebral palsy, seemingly happy-go-lucky announcers are a prime source of enjoyment—but also an accidental source rich in potential for fantasies that often can never be fulfilled. One needs to see that authentic hope imagines real things, things that have some possibility of becoming true.

Reality-based hope, hope that imagines what is actually possible, is most easily achieved when it is experienced in union with another. Some of the best moments in learning or therapy, for example, can be thought of as situations in which two or more people "imagine the possibility," then work together to achieve it. If the words cannot be spoken clearly, the adult and child work together toward alternate ways of achieving the speech clarity wanted; if the word cannot be decoded from the written page, adult and child consider alternate ways of coming to terms, of learning to manage the materials; if the standard method or material proves inadequate for a particular child's needs, an act of imagination may be called for. In such instances, an act of faith—the adult's in the child, the child's in the adult, and the child's and adult's together in the process—is required; this act of faith is the twin of hope.

For hope to be reality-based certain components must be present. First, one must be able to take the view that the problem can be solved—if this possibility cannot be recognized, it is unlikely that one would take action. Second, one must believe that appropriately effective ways exist for achieving that which is desired. Third, one must feel that there is at least one other who is not only interested but has some capacity to participate helpfully in effecting the desired change. In the context of parent counseling, the parents must view the counselors as willing and able to participate. Counselors need a feeling of conviction about the procedures they employ. The one factor that correlates with psychotherapeutic success is the degree to which all participants have faith in the treatment practiced. It seems that regardless of therapeutic technique, this faith in one's method is the one ingredient most consistently linked with therapeutic success. Parents, sensing this faith in workers, their children, or themselves, are more likely to feel more optimistic about outcomes; this feeling of optimism, itself, has therapeutic value.

Sometimes we find it difficult, perhaps impossible for a time, to hope, to imagine the possibilities. Mr. Winters, for example, was a hard-driving businessman who, during one of our parent group discussions of hope, impatiently declared, "What a joke. Hope is only a word. We need hard facts and real techniques to deal with these problems. Hope cannot be proven to exist in any scientific way. I'm not sure the idea of discussing hope has any validity in this tough world." Mrs. Warren, a former teacher with a hearing-impaired daughter and a son diagnosed as dyslexic, responded, "I have never touched hope any more than I have touched God, but both are as real to me as the flowers that grow in my garden."

Hope is best realized when it occurs as shared communion with others: husband with wife, parent with child, child with teacher, counselor with parent. Shared hope can be the basis for the most creative communication, the most fruitful relationship. On the other hand, to be alone or to feel completely alone or defeated can threaten hope. "I've given up on trying to help him with his homework—we always end up angry and yelling," says one mother. "Nothing I do can please my mother," says one child. "I give up."

Such situations call not only for hope, but for courage, too. It may take courage for an adult to try a new way of interacting with a child; it may take even greater courage for a child to attempt something at which he feels he may—again—fail. In such moments courage, faith, and hope may become indistinguishable.

It is remarkable how seldom the quality of hope is talked about. Paul Tillich, the Protestant theologian, wondered why it was that so few of today's philosphers and theologians ever write of hope. Psychologists and educators, it seems to me, hardly ever do. Perhaps because hope is not seen as a clear, distinct idea, and because it cannot be objectively or scientifically measured, it is rendered suspect for valid professional inquiry. And while it can be argued that without hope life could become an empty affair, it can also be argued that our hopes frequently fool and even betray us. They may mislead us after a long line of illusions. Hope can be the maker of despair or what H. L. Mencken once termed the "pathological belief in the occurrence of the impossible."

Hope sometimes appears in the garb of the wishful anticipation or expectation that "things will get better—somehow." One hopes in a way suggestive of magic—things will get better: (1) when we move, (2) now that he has a new teacher, (3) through God's guidance, (4) now that the weather is warm and he can go out, (5) if we just give it enough time. Here lies the wish for fulfillment without real investment, without personal effort. Sometimes magical hope is resigned or passive. It may be a conscious or subconscious thing. It may even occur as an angry demand: "I've done all I can! Now we deserve a better fate!" Occasionally magical hope masks a suppressed despair. As in instances of chronic depression, the individual may be rendered relatively immobile, unable or reluctant to make use of sound reason, to dig into discovering causes or new adjustments, unable simply to act. In not a few instances magic-hope may be accompanied by superstitions. Once in a while one meets a person who never lives, but only hopes to live.

We notice, too, the correlation between feelings such as hope and the physical health of the individual. Editor and publisher Norman Cousins once observed that words like hope, faith, grace, and love do not represent mere vague processes of the human spirit; they also have their physiological significances. These benevolent emotions are useful for the usual reasons, but also because they are regenerative. Cousins realized that the will to live produces a responsive chemistry.

Hope—realistic hope—can be the wellspring of life's search for meaning, the spur to greater achievement, the driving force that enables us to turn dreams into reality. However, realistic hope includes consciousness of the boundaries of our dreams, boundaries that separate the certainty from the possibility. Realistic hope recognizes and accepts the world as it is. We see the possibilities of both joy and tragedy, but within these boundaries hope strengthens the endurance needed to discover meaning and value in life as we experience it. The father of a retarded boy expressed it this way:

For years I just wanted the whole thing to go away, you know? Like I was looking for a cure all the time. Now I know better. In Italian we have a saying: *poco a poco*—little by little. Now that's what I do. I go for a little at a time. I have big goals, you know, but in a day-by-day situation, I'm satisfied with little gains. That way it's better for Joey, too. And once in a while we make a touchdown. Yes, we all do.

Creative living and counseling try to point up the positive features and possibilities of the present. Strengths more than weaknesses in parents or children are stressed. The creative impulse tries to stir a sense of what is possible. It does so in a way that enlarges the goodness of the present in relation to an attainable future such as occurs in the setting up of realistic goals and the growth experience of working together to reach them. It will take deep support from others and courage from within oneself to try new ways, break fixed belief systems, go beyond nondevelopmental security, to take the risks involved in creative insecurity. To hope is to come to believe, as William James long ago observed, that the pull of the future is as real as the push from behind.

Every parenthood has a history, part of which is hope. One begins parenthood with the hope that one will be success-ful. Similarly, every other relationship begins with the hope that it will be successful. When we begin anything, hope must be present, for without the hope that promises the probability of completion, we might not begin at all.

Both parents and allied workers are searchers—seekers of the good hope fulfilled. Could we again describe our search as mutual—a search for inventing ourselves in creative rela-tionship with others? I believe so. Yes, there are the other searchings—for the better school, the more understanding doctor, the accurate diagnosis, the correct method. We are familiar with these understandable searches that parents go through. Often the search is simply for a glimmer of hope. Hope is, for some, the key ingredient to human survival; hope is neither lost nor abandoned.

As for those who work with impaired children, the wisest of them have no wish to have the children think or act exactly as they do. But professionals do, I believe, have in mind an image of what children can become. It must be an image based in large measure on hope, but hope that has solid linkage to the facts. It is an image that also contains a hope of what parents can become through the best possible relationships with their children and each other.

It has been difficult to speak of *hope* without *hopelessness* suggesting itself. But where was it ever promised us that life would be simple, free from pain and doubt? The purpose of life is not simply to be contented. The purpose of life is to have it make a difference that we lived at all, to matter to someone. Ourselves in relationship with a special child can be purpose, can make a difference. Within that fact lies our hope and the child's. Life needs hope to continue and grow. In acts both great and small can hope reside; the planting of a seed is a labor of hope; the baking of a cake is; so, too, is the beginning of a walk in the park or along the shore.

In our sometimes wearying efforts we need to be sustained by hope, with its vision of a lovelier and better world. This is a hope that is not fantasy, for the possibilities of advance in our children, in ourselves, in the world are as unlimited as the possibilities of failure and hurt. The nature of our visions and the direction of our travels will depend on what we do *now*.

May my speech be one with my mind,
And my mind be one with my speech.

Upanishads

COMMUNICATING

In a significant sense, if persons cannot communicate they die of loneliness. Any serious disruption in communication constitutes a little death. To communicate means to be in relationship with another; *not* to communicate means to be out of relationship with another. While speech is the most uniquely human aspect of human fuctioning and the primary method of interpersonal communication, nonverbal processes are also critical; those processes, like works of art, communicate what lies beyond ordinary language.

Communication can hurt, confuse, or serve to increase love, joy, feelings of self-worth. Families can communicate too many hurting things, or at least more than what is consciously intended. Or they do not communicate enough; too often important things remain unspoken. Where impaired children are concerned, communication is especially significant. It is helpful, from time to time, to remind ourselves of the gift most of us have, the gift of communicating, especially through language:

We walked down the path to the well-house, attracted by the fragrance of the honeysuckle with which it was covered. Someone was drawing water and my teacher placed my hand under the spout. As the cool stream gushed over one hand, she spelled into the other the word "water" first slowly, then rapidly. I stood still, my whole attention fixed upon the motion of her fingers. Suddenly, I felt a mystic consciousness as of some thing forgotten, a thrill of returning thought, and somehow the mystery of language was revealed to me. I knew then that water meant the wonderfully cool something that was flowing over my hand. That living word awakened my soul, gave it light, hope, joy, set it free!*

With these inspirational words, Helen Keller in *The Story of My Life* reminded us of the gift that not all receive and not enough use wisely—the gift of words. It has been said that the limits of one's language are the limits of one's world. Perhaps, but the clear ring of truth in that belief is known to any parent whose child cannot speak or read or write, or who can do so only after great effort. To be able to communicate efficiently is to be able to come into significant relationship with others, with vast sources of knowledge, and with the world in which we live.

Most communication consists of dialogue. Let us look at dialogue again from the view of one of this century's most important representatives of the human spirit, Martin Buber. In his poetic book, *I and Thou*, Buber distinguished between an *I-Thou* relationship, which is a direct, mutual openness between persons, and an *I-It* relationship, in which one treats the other only indirectly and nonmutually, perhaps manipulatively. I-It dialogue is necessary in the world, but must not predominate in our movements toward healthy communication and personal relationships. In these two forms of relationship, we find concern with the difference between mere existence and authentic life, between being human at all and being more fully human, between being impersonal or self-centered and moving toward wholeness through greater awareness of others and fuller responsiveness to them.

In another of his books, *Between Man and Man*, Buber distinguished among three types of dialogue which I have adapted and found useful in counseling parents. *Technical dialogue* is prompted solely by the need of objective under-

*Excerpt from *The Story of My Life* by Helen Keller. Reprinted by permission of Doubleday & Co., Inc. (New York, 1954, p. 36).

standing; it makes no pretense of relating to the other as a *Thou.* Much of television advertising could serve as example: Very little concern may be shown for the truth or accuracy of what is communicated to the audience. In technical dialogue there is an overconcern with the "techniques" of communication; there are persons who speak fluently and with proper enunciation and pronunciation, but who say little of real content or feeling. Parents with perfectionistic strivings who have attributed unusual value to "proper speaking habits" and perhaps have had training or interest in drama sometimes will seek aid for the "speech problems" of their children when, in fact, the speech is quite in keeping with age-appropriate behavior.

In the second form, *monologue disguised as dialogue,* the participants are physically together but speak in strangely twisted and roundabout ways. An example is one father in a counseling group who makes a point of memorizing everyone else's names and flattering them so that they not only think he cares about them personally, but will like him also. Such persons, as T. S. Eliot has stated, put on a face to meet the faces that they meet. They are *seeming* persons rather than *being*—much less *becoming*—persons. Discussions of this nature are suggestive of theatre of the absurd scripts. Most of us know a person who will speak and, after we respond, will continue speaking as though we hadn't spoken at all; he simply goes on from where he had left off.

In *genuine dialogue,* on the other hand, the participants open themselves to the otherness of their companions. The others are kept in mind in their present and particular being and are attended to with the purpose of establishing a living mutual relationship. Genuine or authentic dialogue may be verbal or silent. It does not always mean love; it may mean anger. But it is direct, honest, and personal—and *confirms* the humanness of the other even while opposing or differing from him. One can enter genuine dialogue only to the extent that one is a maturely real person.

What is required for parents *or* their impaired children to communicate—regardless of social or therapeutic structure or setting, especially in those parent-child relationships that are disordered by hurting feelings or attitudes? Although techniques will vary with circumstances, I am convinced that the following conditions contribute to the development of genuine dialogue or communication:

1. Whatever helps us to feel freer, share ourselves, and affect others in socially desirable ways.
2. Whatever helps us to come closer to others, touch them and be touched in any humanizing sense.
3. Whatever helps us to live with greater joyful spontaneity, nonverbally and verbally.
4. Whatever increases our feelings of hope, faith, and trust in others and in ourselves.
5. Whatever increases our willingness to risk complete living, the courage to be ourselves fully.
6. Whatever increases our feelings of personal worth, and our ability to love and be loved.

Things are not as good between my husband and me as they might appear in public. I know that I became less responsive to him just before going to sleep each night. How could I tell him I was afraid of having another handicapped child? So now he's cold and we are really apart as far as expressing intimate feelings are concerned. Now he's angry and I guess I'm angrier, too. Now he just drops into bed and doesn't even kiss me good night. Maybe—maybe if he'd just tap me on the shoulder some night, a pat on the bottom, something that might get us going again. But he doesn't and—it's crazy—but I don't either.

The relationship of marriage has many bonds, many strands. When these strands are strong and soundly interwoven, life—even in the presence of tragic disability—can be worth the living. There are the shared experiences, the loyalties, the many kinds of love, the cooperations, the likes and dislikes allowed, the memories, the meetings, the habits and surprises, the closeness. To maximize the positive possibilities requires frequent if not constant concern and effort. Individual relationships will require unique adjustments.

The Millers, for example, were members of one of our clinic's wife-husband team discussion groups. They had decided that they didn't really have time enough to talk things over. Mr. Miller, who sold stereo equipment, jokingly suggested that he could leave a tape recorder home with his wife to speak to. He was surprised when we suggested doing exactly that, and we encouraged Mrs. Miller to take five minutes at the end of the day to record her impressions of the day—her thoughts and feelings. She did and soon discovered that somehow she felt better after these sessions. A short time later, the Millers started making recordings of some of their discussions, which they called "the conversation of the week." They were delighted to realize that they not only felt better after these sessions, they also shared more and greater insight about themselves and their relationship. As an extra bonus, they started a file of recordings that they look forward to listening to in future years. This procedure is not appropriate for everyone, but for the Millers, it worked—in part because *they* worked.

Most of us learn to read, but it might often be the case that it is more important for us know how to *listen.* We spend very little time learning how to listen or in listening. And yet, to comprehend a speaker's intent or meaning—be that speaker child, parent, or worker—to be able to read the speaker's voice, so as to know his attitude or feeling, is clearly a critical element in successful human relationships. Even though we spend a thousand times as much energy in speaking as in writing, schools today spend practically no time in cultivating speaking and listening abilities. A pity!

Sometimes, however, words just get in the way of what we deeply want to say. In Nikos Kazantzakis's *Zorba the Greek,* after the bookish young boss talks at length in lofty language, the earthy Zorba replies, "Ah, if only you could dance all that you've just said, then I'd understand." Most of us are lucky enough to enjoy a few blessed moments in our lives when we have the good sense not to speak but simply to act. One of my lucky moments concerned six-year-old Laurel. Dashing home in the rain from school, she had been struck by a car, suffered brain injury with resulting aphasia, partial paralysis, and loss of speech. Now she was completing several months of language therapy at our speech and hearing center. She had progressed nicely. On this particular day she limped into my office with a handful of dandelions she had just picked on a recess walk along the river with her speech therapist. She was set back a bit, I could see, when she spotted the rose atop my desk. I removed the rose from its vase and placed it in a pencil holder, then arranged the dandelions in the vase, smiling appreciatively at their beauty. She grinned happily, then—hearing her therapist call—turned quickly and left. Sometimes silence speaks clearly. The incident reminded me of a story I had read long ago: A Buddhist master was lecturing to some monks; just before the sermon was to begin, a bird in a tree outside the monastery window began singing. The master said nothing. All listened silently. When the bird stopped, the master declared that the sermon was over and he left.

Nevertheless, there are other times when we wish for someone to talk to and with. Of course, parents can sometimes lean on their own parents. A great source of support, understanding, and wisdom are other parents of special children. One young mother of a physically handicapped child told me of her feelings of isolation and depression, of feeling alone with her child, alone with her sad feelings. Visiting a relative who lived in the next state, she was invited to a morning discussion group of young mothers. She enjoyed her visit enormously. "It was great," she explained. "I didn't think I could actually enjoy talking about it!" Upon returning home, she started investigating and discovered several families with physically handicapped young children and began her own morning discussion group. With this sharing came mutual assistance, emotional catharsis and support, and even occasional inspiration. This group gradually became a persuasive force in their community for the causes of children with special needs.

Another group, parents of adolescents with serious impairments, met recently for one of their semiannual meetings. Their communicative links were many—personal, supportive, social, informational, legal, community, professional—developed over eight years. I was reminded that the dialogue one hears at a meeting of parents of older children often differs from that heard with parents of very young children. For example, the father of a seventeen-year-old, emotionally impaired boy commented:

I'm amazed at the strength of the parent instinct, I really am. Your kid may get into drugs, take your money, commit robbery, yet the parent instinct makes you protect them. You'd never do that for anybody else, maybe not even for your wife, but for your children you do. You have to stay together or else you're nowhere. One moment I think he's an animal and the next I think he's a great guy. Yes, when nature put in the instincts, the parent instinct must have been the first and the strongest.

Another parent responded:

It's good to be able to share—including the pain—especially with someone who's been there—who knows where you're at. And I share their heartaches, too. But now I'm starting to share some laughs, also. At first I felt guilty—even making jokes up about the kid, you know—we all do that sometimes. But I'm getting a better overall look at things. Yet I couldn't do it alone.

The mother of a child who had both a congenital hearing loss and severely deformed leg was speaking of her son:

He is hampered. Not quite so free to move, to jump, run, to play. He's not able to climb a mountain or to dance or fight as well. He's got an artificial limb, and even that could break down. And when he looks in a mirror he can't see a whole person—it'll be rough. What about girls, getting married? No, he'll always be less than what he could have been.

This boy's father continued:

Yeh, but all of this is basically his suffering, not ours. Of course, I'll admit I suffer for myself in terms of what I expected—what I hoped for in a son. But that's the suffering that goes with a loss like this. I suffer because he's got to, but also because I myself have had a loss. Yet, what have we lost? Only something I imagined. What have we gained? Leg or not, a son and, let's face it—I love him and we'll go on from here—and, oh yes, maybe he'll climb a mountain—a little smaller one, maybe.

Throughout these writings, I have referred to parent *groups*. The value of group activities to all spheres of communications and relationships can be immense. While therapeutic group structures vary greatly, most offer parents these helpful components:

1. A commonality of concerns.
2. A source of acceptance, friendship, love.
3. A source of possible insight and increased awareness of one's self and relationships with others.
4. A time to increase one's problem-solving approach and ability.
5. A focus on daily here-and-now issues.
6. A chance to receive corrective feedback from others.

71367

7. An opportunity to try out new ways of thinking, feeling, and relating.
8. A safe place for emotional "letting go."
9. A chance to observe others as models of behaviors, or to be a model for others.
10. An opportunity to realize that one is not unique with one's problems or alone in the world.

In group counseling that is psychotherapeutically oriented, quite commonly at the outset we observe the following characteristics, especially in those family relationships more significantly disturbed:

1. Participants do not communicate clearly with one another; thoughts and feelings are expressed in distorted fashion or are misinterpreted.
2. Participants are not in effective touch with their own feelings, or in fact deny feelings they actually do have.
3. Participants treat exceptionability or differentness as guilt-connected, threatening, or conflict-connected.
4. Participants deal unrealistically with each other or situations: things are wished for or fearfully expected, rather than dealt with in their context in the here-and-now, or in terms of hope that has some possibility of fulfillment.
5. Participants deny responsibility for what they feel or do, attributing what happens to circumstances or others.

When counseling is moving along well, a progression of the following kind is observed, time spans varying considerably: Most parents, at the outset, ask direct questions, seek specific *information*. They want to know what to do, how to do it, and when. A shift occurs to a *sharing* phase in which suggestions are discussed and exchanged, emphases being on technique. Gradually, a *feeling* phase develops; participants examine their own and others' feelings and attitudes and try to see how these are related to their behaviors with significant others. Insights are related to the larger family, to neighbors, friends, and community.

Perhaps in all such group meetings, in all dialogue which is *I-Thou* associated, the key feature is that the individual is in helpful relationship, is not alone. For example, one may discover that loneliness does not arise from the absence of people about one, but from not having sufficient resources to communicate the things that seem important.

Another way to say that one is not alone is to refer to the common ground one discovers in relationship. When people have an opportunity to go to the depths of their own experiences, then bring these intimate emotions to the surface, though perhaps shocked for a time at their impulses, they eventually discover themselves to be in concert with a large company of individuals with similar experiences.

In deeply personal communication, we discover nothing new and unknown in other human beings, even disordered ones; rather, we encounter the most elemental structures of our own natures. One father admitted that all of his life he had been antagonistic to minority groups. One evening, after two years of participating in sessions with parents representing several racial and ethnic groups, he shared these words with us:

I know now that we are alike in many ways, perhaps in the most important ways. We all feel pain and sadness. We're all struggling to make the most of our lives. We want the best for our children. We need love and recognition ourselves, each of us. We sometimes feel alone, but we bless any chance to laugh out loud, to have a share of happiness. And we all have kids with different problems. We have a lot in common.

To communicate ideally, fully, authentically is to live fully. All that is spoken of in this work is related intimately to communicative effectiveness—hope, trust, love, daring, knowing, feeling, being honest, and all the other necessities for vital living. Part of the gift of healthy communication is this: Every person's vision of the world expands to the degree that he or she is able to see through the eyes of another. Some help us to see their vision of the world through speech, others through song or dance, work or play; not a few are most comfortable, or perhaps most communicative, through writing. The mother of an eight-year-old, nonverbal child, shy herself, handed me these lines she had written about her child; she said that she had wanted to share them with the group but was not quite ready:

It is a wondrous thing
that if you but touch my hand
with naught but your small finger

or if you smile at me—
silent but with eyes that warmly speak;

I become Laughter, Light and Happiness;
No longer alone am I;
I become a world, a Life.

Writing as therapy has a very long history. I have found writings to be a valuable counseling medium, not only for parents but for their children as well. In relation to the question, "Who are you?" student clinicians collected responses such as these from families with whom they worked:

1. The mother of a deaf girl who had overcome a serious childhood illness: "I am a fallen leaf who waited for the wind to lift me up again."
2. An emotionally disturbed high-school girl: "I am the guitar string you plucked too hard and broke."
3. A father who regularly beat his bully son: "I am the boss and that's it."

4. A twelve-year-old boy with muscular dystrophy: "I am a snowflake melting in your hand."
5. A fifteen-year-old girl with severe cleft palate and harelip: "I am a princess masquerading as a frog."
6. A brilliant high-school student who stuttered severely: "I am a song waiting to be sung."

Healthy communication recognizes and accepts those experiences and needs we all share. A creative parent recognizes personal limitations; so does the creative counselor. Both parent and counselor have this need to recognize in common. Creative counselors realize the impossibility of being as knowledgeable about some areas of exceptional human behavior as others; range and complexity are too great. They recognize the difficulty of being as helpfully sensitive and comfortable with some feelings, relationships, and problem areas as with others. Creative counselors can encourage freedom of expression and spontaneity only to the degree to which they themselves are capable of such expression; they can show attitudes of trust and faith in the capacity of those they counsel to the extent that they, themselves, genuinely feel that trust in themselves. The sharing of such realizations between counselors and parents need not always occur fully. However, movement toward such sharing is highly desirable, and parents and counselors aware of and functioning in accord with those realizations tend to achieve maximum growth in the relationship. This kind of healthy communication also constitutes a desirable model for parents for their own interactions within the family.

Creative parenting, like creative counseling, is a voyage of self-discovery, a journey to a wider horizon of conscious awareness of self and others. It recognizes what each one of us peculiarly *is,* what we prize, what we hope for, and how we search for fuller humanness; but it is also alert to discover that which we share, our humanity.

In all instances of creative living, healthy communication serves as a foundation. And for most of life's situations, the smallest numerical combination is two—a pair; we cannot exist fully except in relationship with another, in helping communication with another. Life's journey is often a long one in which we experience frustration, doubt and some joy. In our efforts to help children, we—parents, counselors, siblings—need to know techniques, but these are insignificant unless caught by a vision that enables them to soar beyond the commonplace. Techniques, methods, and materials can be dead things until fired by human spirit.

Well, then, what do we want in communication? May we for now say this: We want—between or among parents, children, workers, neighbors, friends—communication which is as intelligible as possible, but which is also courteous, civilized; which is sociable, curious, tolerant, suspicious of radical views; which is not interested in advancing at the expense of another; which is open, honest, and kind with others and self; which is simple without naiveté; and, which has courage and love in it.

Too idealistic, you say? Reaching for the stars? Well, the stars, it is true, cannot be touched, but they guide us just the same. And was it not Browning who said, "Ah, but man's reach should exceed his grasp,/Or what's a heaven for?"*

Let us conclude this section by recognizing that the ability to speak, to use language, to communicate does not depend on being intelligent, on having a large brain, on being highly trained; it depends upon being *human*. To communicate well—to speak, to write, to relate well—is to live most fully. Our role as parent or counselor is to help some of our more needy fellow-travelers on this planet to live well. Then they and we will communicate better.

*From "Andrea del Sarto" (1855).

God guard me from the thoughts men think
In the mind alone.
He that sings a lasting song
Thinks in a marrowbone.

William Butler Yeats, "A Prayer for Old Age."

FEELING

One day many, many years ago, I was lucky enough as a graduate student to be strolling in the yard of the John Tracy Clinic in Los Angeles with Louise Tracy, who had founded the clinic in her son's name. Two hearing-impaired three-year-old children ran up to us as we were seriously pondering an educational problem. They appeared to sense our momentary concentration and skipped off happily elsewhere. "They seem to understand that we need to be left alone for a few minutes," I said. "Of course they understand," Mrs. Tracy replied. "They listen with their hearts."

It is helpful, as parent or worker, to discover early that attitudes and feelings are more important than facts; that it is not facts, but what we believe about those facts which shapes our behavior. Stated differently, what we think about children or others, the value of things large or small, depends on the feelings they stir in us. Human individuality is founded on *feeling*. It is in the deeper realms of *feeling* that we find real fact, immediately sense how things happen. Our most intense feelings occur not in terms of ourselves alone but in deep response to another. Life without feeling would not be life at all.

But many of us find it difficult to express true feelings, all the more if we are uncertain about how others will respond. Most of us can recall a moment when we looked at a friend, our spouse, a parent, or child, and a surge of love and appreciation swept over us, but somehow something kept us from expressing ourselves to the other; we remained silent and the moment passed. Or at a social gathering, we heard some gossip that derogated an absent person; we resented the disrespect but said nothing, then felt embarrassed at our lack of courage. At a restaurant we see a child with severe cerebral palsy, his body writhing and jerking erratically. But his parents are lovingly determined that the evening out will be a success. Their management and mood during the meal are marvelous, and we feel an urge to go over and say, "I think you're all wonderful." But we are likely to go on with our own meal, saying nothing at all to them.

Why do we so fear open expression? Usually we are afraid of what might happen if we expressed our true feelings. Others might be embarrassed; we might be. Or we may be regarded suspiciously and made to look ridiculous. So we stay behind our masks. We remain linked to the so-called logical, sensible, and realistic part of ourselves, the part that is related to control, restrictions, taboo, the laws of the physical world, the abstract symbolic. We neglect what has become a far country, the world of emotion—of crying, laughter, and love; it is childlike experience, though not childish; it is that part of our concrete selves closest to raw experience; it is the individual world of fantasy, imagination, wishes, and magic. Henry David Thoreau, in his unique way, seemed to speak of these differing domains of human experience when he wrote in his *Journals:*

We seem to linger in manhood to tell the dreams of our child-hood, and they vanish out of memory as we learn the language.

The mother of an autistic son and deaf daughter spoke to the point quite directly:

I think, think, think. If I could only feel, feel, feel.

Somehow, many of us have consciously forgotten that we were *feeling* creatures long before we were *thinking* ones; the mind is younger than the heart. The head does not hear until the heart has listened; what the heart knows today the head may understand tomorrow. In some life situations, perhaps only feeling truly comprehends feeling. As I write these words, a clinical incident comes to my mind: Mrs. Martin met me in the clinic corridor and asked me if she could sit in my office for a while. I opened my door for her and she entered, sat down, and burst into tears. I closed the door and sat down myself, saying nothing.

It was obvious that she simply needed to cry. Mrs. Martin's husband had suffered a stroke one year before, leaving her with full responsibility not only for his care but for their three preschool children as well. Now Mrs. Martin had recently learned that she herself had an inflammatory disorder, lupus erythematosus. As she continued crying, and I thought of her total life situation, I found myself quietly weeping. Our eyes met and I gently embraced her for a minute or two. Gradually her weeping subsided. She dried her tears, raised her head, and returned to the waiting room. No words had been spoken, but enough had been said.

The heart-mind, feeling-thought continuum is referred to in a lovely way in one of my favorite little books, *Jung and Hesse: A Record of Two Friendships,* by Miguel Serrano, the Chilean writer and diplomat. Serrano, recounting a discussion with Dr. Jung in 1959, tells the following story: Jung spoke of a conversation he had had with the chief of the Pueblo Indians, whose name was Ochwiay Biano, which means "mountain lake." The chief had given his impressions of white men, saying that they were always upset, always searching for something, and, as a result, their faces were lined with wrinkles, which he viewed as a sign of eternal restlessness. Ochwiay Biano also felt that white people were crazy since they believed that they thought with their heads, and it was well known that crazy people did that. The chief, asked by Jung how *he* thought, replied that naturally he thought with his heart.

To move more deeply into the realm of feeling can be

threatening, but therein lies the possibility of enrichment, too. Among lessons I have learned from parents are these: That self-discovered truths are more likely to endure; and that counseling or education has most potential for human good when it is responsive to the deeper needs, curiosities, wishes, or fantasies of those involved. Some of the most productive moments in counseling occur when parents take the lead in thinking, feeling, and relating their way to a happier, more productive relationship with their children, when they can somehow connect their interactions with their children to a deep wellspring of motivation of their very own. Let me give an illustration:

One counseling group, consisting of four parent couples of young impaired children, had experienced a long period of expressed frustration and anger, but had not managed to move beyond those experiences to more adaptive behaviors. At one point Mrs. Miller said, "I've been reading Elizabeth Kubler-Ross's work, *On Death and Dying,* and it's been helpful to us in adjusting to my father's situation. Dad was angry at first, as I was. Now he is less so. Kubler-Ross talks about stages of grieving. I wonder if we go through the same stages after we realize we have a handicapped child?" This discussion led each group member to read part of Dr. Kubler-Ross's writings and use it as a basis for discussion of his or her own reactions to having a handicapped child. This led in turn to a most intense series of meetings, full of insight, where the parents, indeed, did come to see very close parallels between the two life events. They spoke of their initial reaction of shock and denial, anger, "bargaining" (the unrealistic wish for a cure, miracle, or improvement), and final acceptance of the reality. I can recall Mrs. King at one point saying, "Jamie will be our only child, and he is a handful. Sometimes I think that death would be easier to handle, because it has a finality to it. Sometimes I have wondered if it would have been better if he had died."

Parents of handicapped children will not be surprised or shocked at such statements. What is amazing is that most parents work their way through such issues with surprising courage, though not a little pain. The wonderment I have of how people derive the strength to cope as well as they do with their handicapped children still constitutes a major reason for my continuing involvement in this field. Trying to discover the wellsprings for these sources of deep strength is a part of the search for meaning that constitutes a vital life center for me. The mother of a child with terminal cancer took this view:

I have to stop thinking of childhood as a means to some end— and start thinking of it as an end in itself; to be treasured and respected in itself.

Some time later, after her child had died, this mother spoke to one of our evening parent meetings:

Focus on the happy times. Don't waste precious time. Or else waste time in a happy way, with no guilt. Convert that emotional energy into creative activities for the family and yourself. You have to face up to the feelings that come—the disappointment, the anger, the guilt. Cry or talk it out in the presence of a supporting person—sometimes you'll do it alone. And it will also be necessary to encourage your child to talk out his own feelings, or express them in *some* way, like play. People sometimes behave as though we're not supposed to indulge ourselves in sorrow. Don't let that faze you. Don't care. Because sometimes we do feel sorrow—feel it deeply. None of us can deny it. After all, it happened to us, not them.

Adjusting to the negative feelings expressed by some people toward special children can be challenging to parents. The handicap itself, if it is a publicly observable, severe one, will be an object of curiosity to many, occasionally evoking either their pity or their aversion; such persons may find it difficult to be at ease in the child's presence. The child frequently senses their discomfort and may react with anger, hurt, or withdrawal. People who are unsure of themselves in the presence of special children may overreact, possibly embarrassing the child or his parents with their excessive concern or by pretending to ignore the impairment. Even if the special child is too young to make such discriminations, his parents will have sensed these behaviors, and the child will be affected indirectly by their reactions. Such occurrences may lead to stress in maintaining a good balance between anxious concern and overprotection. In more extreme instances, where the parents are disappointed in their assumed "failure" to have brought forth, like their friends, a perfectly normal child, some inclination toward rejection of the child or of themselves may crop up.

And a kind of perfection is what some parents seem to seek; all should be "normal." If there is trouble between family members, they seem to be saying it "should not be." Peace and quiet must reign. Any irritants are to be resolved by talking, good humor, or sufficient self-discipline. Anger is regarded as unnatural; if something is wrong, then more effort and intelligence on everyone's part will right the difficulty. Such rules, when rigidly adhered to, must eventually lead to enormous anxiety and guilt.

While there are rough spots in any relationship, there are also positive values in frustration, anger, and release. For every parent, more or less, there will be moments of anger, times when everything is going wrong and the children still demand attention. It is a very unusual parent who will not occasionally lose emotional control:

If I feel very emotional, then I'd usually better express it. If I have an idea that my anger is due not to my children but to my own sense of frustration, I try to temper it a bit. And if I can, I damned well let them know exactly why I'm angry. Then at least they'll know where they stand—I think they deserve that, knowing where they stand. And knowing that parents have rights, too. Then, in a quiet moment later, I'll try to figure out what it really was that upset me, try to learn about myself.

Brothers and sisters of special children have special feelings, too. This topic deserves a book in itself, but let us at least say this: Siblings of special children also need opportunities to talk or play out raw feelings—jealousy about the special child's privileges or attentions; guilt about not being handicapped, or about not doing enough for the other child; a sense of family stigma; embarrassment; anger; or feelings of friendship and love. Said the brother of a dying child:

Every so often he loses his cool with me for no reason I can see. Out of frustration I suppose. Sometimes I get this feeling of resentment about the things I'm able to do and he's not, like I'm more and more into life and he's—well, he's more and more out of it. Who could blame him?

Some time later the same young man, who had devoted much time to the care of his brother, expressed these feelings:

Sometimes I'd feel angry, though I wouldn't express it, because I felt so tied down. Sometimes I'd get terrifically angry and feel like yelling out something, like, "Damn you! You're the cause of my being trapped and lonely. You've made life hard for me!" But I never did—out loud.

The feelings of special children themselves also deserve a separate book. The feeling of guilt, for example, is not rare. As I recall children experiencing guilt, phrases such as these come to mind: "If I could walk/hear/see/learn, my parents wouldn't have a problem." "If I had been O.K. . . . , my father might still be with us." "If I had not been born. . . ." "Maybe my parents are staying together just because of me. . . ."

Sometimes guilt meets guilt if parents, too, harbor feelings of self-blame: "I drove myself too hard." "I was too demanding." "We've been poor parents." "We did something wrong." "I didn't notice soon enough." "I didn't get help soon enough." "I got the wrong kind of help."

Occasionally, we meet parents who are consistently oversensitive to what others think—about them, their children, their methods of bringing up children, their treatment of their special child. They remind one of Arthur Miller's play, *Death of a Salesman,* in which the hero, caring too deeply whether others like him, lives so as never to displease anyone. Not even for a good cause can he risk being disliked. Parents who are out of touch with their feelings in this way sometimes go to the extreme of playing the martyr's role, partially to elicit the sympathy of others. They have reminded me from time to time of Jung's comment on one of his patients: "He did a great deal of good—far too much—and as a result was usually irritable." An old German saying also comes to mind: "Everybody's friend is everybody's fool." While teaching in Italy recently, I came across this phrase, also appropriate: *Tanto buon che vale niente* ("So good he is good for nothing").

In certain circumstances, it would be unreal for a parent not to be irritated. Mrs. Deno's son, seventeen years old, is emotionally disturbed and attends a residential school, occasionally coming home on weekends. Regardless of the cause of his deviant behavior, when he is at home he consistently is very hard to get along with. Recently, Mrs. Deno was talking about his visits:

When Billy is home on weekends, he's got to be constantly on the go. We try to do everything he'd like, you know. But he'll usually get bored and he'll say, "I want to go back to the Center. It's lousy here." Makes me feel like a rotten parent. I might say, in a controlled way, you know, "O.K. let's get ready." But inside I'm saying, "You ungrateful bugger!"

And are there not those times in the life of every parent when one wishes simply to be quietly alone with one's feelings and thoughts? Such moments are often terribly difficult to come by, for the demands on a parent of a special child can be awesome. But one cannot live perpetually in a state of unending work and responsiveness to others, or one may become torn into a hundred pieces—shattered. For most parents, it is necessary from time to time to exert a conscious effort to oppose the self-scattering forces and to call into action the self-knitting, self-quieting, self-healing ones. Some quiet time alone is necessary—listening to calming music, in prayer or contemplation, a peaceful respite of reading. This centering movement in solitude need not be a momentous act, but it should flow from the inner self and return to the self in an inward attentiveness. True, the centering of one's life around a special child may constitute a legitimate focus, an outer strength, but the inner strengths must not be forgotten.

13
OPENING

If a person does not ascend a high mountain, he will not know the height of heaven.

Hsun Tzu

115

In my courses in psychological language and communication disorders, I sometimes make this request of the students: "Would any of you like to give me your definition of what it means to be 'open'? But give me a nonverbal definition; in other words, use 'body English.'" The reactions I receive to this request vary enormously. Some students rise to a wide stance, raise their arms aloft with palms outstretched and look to the sky; others simply hold out their open hands before them; a few kneel, sitting on their haunches, arms stretched behind toward their toes, head up, eyes open or closed. Not a few are befuddled. Some appear totally incapable of expressing themselves in this way, at least in terms of the word "open." For many persons to "open up" themselves may be dangerous, embarrassing, threatening, in some ways discomforting. I am thinking particularly of some parents who, for various reasons, have become withdrawn, less sociable, fearful of expressing feelings fully because they might be rendered vulnerable. For some, it is as though they were saying, "I've let myself go before, and got slapped for it, made mistakes, was made to look the fool, got hurt, etc." Such situations are particularly unfortunate if parents, because of their child's impairment, withdraw into a kind of protective shell, a shell of martyrdom, a shell of hurt, one of "bravely going it alone," or one of stubborn defiance ("I'll show the world we can make it"). Perhaps it is but a shell of confusion and numbness for a time. Our concern increases when we see that the closing off is becoming chronic, and that the effects on parents, child, and psycho-educational development are becoming increasingly destructive.

If there are key requisites to successful coping with handicapping conditions, one must be an *openness to change* on the part of all involved. *Change* is a crucial element in counseling, as it is in all of life. Change includes an openness, not only on the parents' part but on the counselor's as well—an openness to the possibilities of appropriateness and goodness across a wide continuum of helping procedures. It represents an openness on the parents' part to consider, when necessary, different ways of behaving, thinking, and feeling as mates and as parents. It may include the idea of openness on the part of the impaired child to express more freely with others his deeper feelings, thoughts, wishes, and also to be more receptive to the honestly expressed feelings and thoughts of others. Degree of openness for anyone will vary with the type and degree of emotion; in general, defensiveness closes—spontaneity opens; anxiety closes—confidence opens; humiliation closes—feelings of acceptance and personal worth open; mistrust closes—trust opens; anger closes—love opens.

To open means to express oneself more freely and honestly, to realize that there is an element of risk in behaving that way, but also to know that the effects may be wonderful:

I'm finally doing what I believe in doing for my child. Not everyone agrees with me, but, somehow, I've developed the courage to do what *I* think is right. I get disagreed with, and sometimes criticized. And I'm sure the school authorities and the hospitals think I'm a damned nuisance. I don't mean to be mean. But I'm better in tune with what I think, and I'm expressing those thoughts, because deep in my heart I've got to do what I think is right, regardless of what others say. I think they all liked me better when I was a shrinking violet. Well, I'm hardly that any longer, and we're *all* better off for it.

I asked the mother who wrote these words to me if she could identify a turning point from what had been a deep depression following the birth of her deaf daughter, to a more optimistic outlook. She told me that the family had driven out one weekend to visit the Clarke School for the Deaf when her daughter was about eighteen months old. They had enjoyed a helpful discussion there and then, on the way back to Boston, visited the campus of Mt. Holyoke College; there, on a sundial, they discovered this inscription:

**To a larger sight, the rim of
Shadow is the line of light.**

She continued, explaining that she wasn't sure of a definite turning point, but that this inscription symbolized it for her— from a gloomy outlook to one in which she saw her daughter's deafness as a challenge and an opportunity for family members to live and grow in new ways.

I have said that, for the good of the child, not only must parents sometimes relinquish the defense of closing themselves off—from relationships, from alternatives to present action, from their own true thoughts and feelings; the *workers* who serve children and families of impaired children must also remain open rather than closed systems if maximum service is to be delivered. Again, we observe the commonality of being parent *or* professional—in this instance, in terms of being "open to the possibilities." I'd like to discuss this point a bit more.

One of the greatest dangers professional workers may experience is that of becoming *fixed* in their beliefs or procedures. As with parents, clinicians need to have the courage of their doubts. Any learning in human servicing which involves a fundamental change in self-organization—in the way in which one regards and behaves toward self and others—tends to be threatening and therefore may be resisted. While this is as true for impaired children as it is for their parents, it is likely to be true for counselors as well. Creative counselors do not feel driven to espouse only one point of view, one technique. Nor do they feel that they must strive always for agreement between parents and child; they respect and encourage the personal validity of each individual's view even when they appear conflicting. It is difficult to see how this could be anything else but the case when working with children or parents representing a wide spectrum of both health and dysfunctions. For example, once we found ourselves working with a six-year-old referred to our clinic because of mounting behavior problems. The father, aged thirty-two, suffered a stroke eighteen months before which left him hemiplegic and almost speechless. There are two younger children, and the mother, a mild-mannered person with serious health problems of her own, had always left the "major decisions" up to her husband. Counseling, rehabilitation, and therapy procedures must be greatly varied to suit such a range of family needs, and we "tailored" our services accordingly.

Counselors may find themselves giving direct information; asking very specific questions; acting as arbitrator, interpreter, resource person for allied medical and welfare supportive services, language analyst, accepting supporter, utilizer of nonverbal techniques; and so on. Rigid adherence to set methodology in such circumstances could, to say the least, cause wonderment. Fixed beliefs tend to be noncreative foundations; it behooves us to tolerate, respect, and try to see goodness in the views of others, however unintelligible they may seem to us; neither all of truth nor all of goodness is given to any one person, although each may derive value from a particular perspective. Perhaps all we need is to be faithful to our own situation and opportunities, making the most of them most humanly, without taking it upon ourselves to impress our own views overbearingly upon others.

But to be open, it must be repeated, is to take the risk of being less defensive, or of leaving a secure if nondevelopmental position, for one that may be, at least for a time, much more threatening. Have you ever seen a bird cower in its cage when the door was opened for it to fly free? It is a queer notion to all too many people that in order to find themselves, they first must lose themselves; or, that the greatest insights often follow our giving our less rational natures some free rein.

Mr. Herbert, for example, was a lawyer and father of one of our emotionally immature children; in our weekly parent group meetings, he never was able fully to express real feelings—or to develop much insight about his defensiveness or its relationship to his son's disorder. He could never express himself in more than factual terms, and he was the one individual who did not form a substantial bond with at least one other parent. His involvements were intellectual and fleeting. He eventually disappointed everyone he met, and he found others disappointing, although he remained apparently cheerful and characteristically convinced of his own rightness. He just missed being human. He was quite fluent verbally; he spoke the socially proper words. But he reminded me that it is perfectly possible to speak articulately—even mellifluously—and say absolutely nothing! He was, as T.S. Elliot might have said, a gentleman in the worst sense of the word.

Bill Dunn was another father in the same group. (I find it interesting that while I referred to *Mr.* Herbert, Mr. Dunn I called Bill). Bill was regarded, I believe, as "a simple man." But it was an open and even sublime simplicity, one that prevented extreme self-consciousness. Mr. Herbert was, in a sense, forever thinking about himself, weighing every ponderous word and thought. Bill Dunn was simply himself. Mr. Herbert seemed constantly to worry about having said or done too much or too little. Bill Dunn was at ease with others, frank, unrestrained, and natural. Mr. Herbert was self-absorbed, reserved, self-conscious, uncomfortable at the smallest intrusion into his self-complacency; his was the solemn wisdom of the vain and foolish. Bill Dunn, on the other hand, was more wise, for he was reflective without being out of touch with others, responsive to others without being so merely for his own sake. Mr. Herbert was a closed system; Bill Dunn was an open one.

The father of a nine-year-old boy diagnosed as autistic was in the midst of the struggle between keeping his feelings to himself as he had always done and wanting—but not quite able yet—to finally express a true feeling openly:

I've forgotten, if I ever knew, how to tell my own father that I love him. Now he is dying, and I still cannot tell him. For a dozen weekends I've traveled to be with him, to talk, just to be there. Not simply because he is dying, really, but rather because I want to put my arms round him, to hug him, and to say, "Dad, I love you." But I can't do it. It's awful. And why? Because I think I'll feel silly, embarrassed showing my feelings like that. How crazy it is. Yet, I can't do it.

This father struggled for a long time to break through his strong reserve. It was only after he learned to be more open, more real with his own son—to touch and embrace him, to say that he loved him—that he found the strength to open himself up to his own father, who, indeed, died a short time later.

I finally realized that perhaps my own son felt toward me what I felt toward my own father. I didn't want that to happen again with him, with us. You can say that my son helped me finally to be a true son to my own father. He gave me the courage to be myself.

One of life's strangest paradoxes is that which causes us to stick with a specific condition or situation, even a deeply hurting one, because we cannot bear the tension of venturing into the unknown. And so we stay with the concrete known, unbearable as it is, rather than opening ourselves to the possibilities—the unknown. And yet to me it is a simple fact that when I disclose myself honestly and fully, the mystery that I am clears significantly. And when others disclose themselves to me, the shape of all that I think and feel of them moves closer to their actuality—assuming, of course, that any biases about them, or immature needs of my own, do not interfere with my capacity to have their fullness revealed. Parents who have had the ability to be fully open make statements such as these:

I learned through expressing myself honestly how much I am like other parents, and how much they are like me.

When I opened up, my husband opened up. It wasn't always easy after that, but at least we weren't kidding ourselves.

How can I help my family unless I know what they need? And how can I know what they need unless they tell me? And how can they tell me unless they feel free with me?

Parents who have difficulty opening up to their inner selves may make no statements on the matter, but when they do, they are likely to be statements like these:

To love somebody is a scarey business because you expose yourself. That's when you can be hurt the most. That happened to me. I'm afraid of it happening again.

I was honest about my feelings before. But everyone got down on me for having such thoughts—my husband, my oldest child, my doctor, even the people at church. Now I keep my feelings to myself, and I guess everybody is happier except *me*.

I would rather die than have them know my true thoughts.

I don't have a single person I can be myself with—not one.

I'm considering remarrying. Yet she doesn't know me, really. I've kept most of my feelings about my son and myself to myself. But I'm not being fair to her. It wouldn't be the right kind of love if we did get married and she didn't really know me. Oh, not that I think I should have to reveal every single feeling, but, there is more to me than I have shown—and I'm afraid to show it. Maybe she'll think I'm weak. Yet it would be grand to be with a woman again—in the home—and it would be great for Eddie. Why can't I face up to it?

At the root of mature living is the creativity that faces insecurity as the growing point of life. Parents of impaired children, especially of those severely handicapped, have more chances than most to feel insecure. But such a moment can contain growth potential if it can be regarded as a "creative insecurity." The insecurity of one mother concerned not knowing what the effect would be on her six-year-old, home-bound, cerebral-palsied daughter of not having playmates; she had said that she didn't know what to do. But as soon as this mother thought about and discussed the problem freely, having finally assumed that a good answer was possible, she came up with the idea of inviting neighborhood children to her home from time to time; she prepared ahead, with the help of a recreation therapist, games that would be fun but could allow the inclusion of her daughter, who was soon being invited occasionally to the other children's homes.

The difficulty and the desirability of opening oneself must be encountered by the special child or youth, too. Indeed, a major issue of some handicapping conditions concerns the impaired individual's struggle to function more independently. It is a struggle experienced by both parents and child, and in their relationships. This is particularly true in certain types of handicapping conditions. Let's consider, as an example, the common problem of stuttering. To grow or to improve means opening, taking responsibility, choosing, risking vulnerability, being able to endure the inevitable insecurities. As the stuttering individual increasingly takes the risk of expressing himself more freely and grows stronger in acceptance of any consequences of his action, we see the characteristics of self-creativity revealed. He develops self-reliance; he relinquishes self-derogation, self-defeat. He takes increasing responsibility for his speech behavior, for his own therapy program, for dealing with himself more objectively, for following through on developmental tasks. For a stutterer, like many others, the idea that he himself might have an active part in the direction of his life and of his stuttering can be difficult to accept. Even if environmental factors here played a part in his stuttering, over time, especially by adolescence, the speech problem becomes increasingly *his*. As one speech therapist stated, "He's not guilty because he didn't know better. But now that he knows better he can't keep dodging the responsibility."

Self-reliance means recognizing straightforwardly the part one has played and is still playing in the continuation of the problem and the improved part one can play. We must then help the individual to remove any false fronts, move out of secrecy into openness. But the openness must be genuine. The following note was written by a brilliant college stutterer who was still intellectually defensive:

I am talented in the visual arts—not painting or sculpture—no, in the art of masking—the art of appearance which is disappearance. My stuttering is the mask that keeps me from showing my true face. Of course, masks have their purposes, as do mine.

But stuttering's masks are clever and varied—it's hard to unravel the secret behind; even I may not be truly aware of the mask I wear. It's been said that if you are to understand a Rembrandt self-portrait you must study his entire work and his biography. If you are to understand *my* masterpiece, my stuttering, my mask, perhaps you must study me in my entirety. God! Words, words, words! Another mask?

Another bright young man, deeply beset by and withdrawn because of his severe speech disorder, spoke from a similar view:

You're right, I'm involuted. I must break out into the world. But it will be hard. I've grown so to fear the world. I see its hardness, its cruelty. The price of failure is tremendous. It means contempt and scorn. I'm sensitive. When I'm not accepted I crumble. Will I have the strength to harden myself and, by battling it all, find myself?

To be open, to be creative, means in part to be spontaneous in thought and action. But if one has been hurt time and time again upon expressing oneself spontaneously, one may lose the will to allow one's spontaneity another expression. To be creative means to be able to act freely, but it is difficult to create if one feels physically or psychologically imprisoned. To be open, to be free, means to be free *not* to be safe, to realize that life may be better when one is *least* defended.

This view, I believe, holds as true for the professionals as it does for the impaired individual. Thoughtful workers ask themselves this question: "Should we really make passionate investments in the individuals with whom we work, involve ourselves emotionally, even to the point of possible risk?" The common admonition is: "Don't become emotionally involved." In the best clinical sense, this means the avoidance of satisfying one's deeply personal—much less infantile—needs at the expense of the other person. But in the worst sense it can mean never expressing an emotion that would be truly reflective of one's own feelings. Yet, in many ways, we constantly ask impaired individuals to take the risk of making themselves vulnerable—to do perhaps what they have long avoided doing, to face up to fearful situations, to run the risk of another embarrassment by trying to perform successfully a task always failed previously, and perhaps failing once more. How can we role-play such experiences so as to better appreciate these lives of others? How, indeed, can they role-play us, especially if we but present to them images of perfection? It is easy enough to label a child "uncommunicative," "unresponsive," or "lacking a verbal repertoire." It does not often enough occur to us that the child simply may not want to talk with the likes of us, in the way we want them to talk, or under the conditions in which we find ourselves together.

But how does one let go? We need strong support in order to open up, to risk a jump at all. Another paradox presents itself: There must be strong support in order to open up, to let go. A child lacking strong home support will find it difficult to open up, to take the risky leaps necessary to achieve greater maturity. A child who has not received love at home is impaired in giving love. A parent who is not able to take in love from spouse or child, or finds none to take in, is similarly impaired. One father, recently separated from his wife, in his anguish blurted out these words to the parents of a child discovered to have cancer:

Forget remission! My own kid died of cancer. They *all* do! All your brave gestures will fall down. Get drunk and pour it out—all the rage and frustration—pour it out with a good friend.

Yes, openness can be brutal, too.

Some parents who have found it difficult to express their thoughts and feelings freely to another have discovered their outlet in the act of writing—letters to friends, a diary perhaps. Through writing they find their safety valve, their dam against a flood of remorse or disappointment, their wall against defeat or collapse.

I keep a diary. And I write a little bit each night—it's just for me. Often I write as though my son will see the words. I mention the hopes I have for him. But I mention the doubts, too. Just a little something each night. And somehow, I feel better, it relaxes me.

There are many ways of opening. To be spontaneous in any sense is to open; to loosen one's defenses is to open; to allow any display of one's shortcomings may be; to behave with less reserve, concealment, or secrecy may be. To be wisely strong in belief in oneself or in another may be, as this passage by Herman Hesse from a German volume of his letters suggests:

What I do believe is that I must stand fast at my post, that even if I am driven to despair . . . I must preserve my reverence for life and for the possibility of giving it meaning, even if in this belief I should find myself alone and make myself ridiculous. To this creed I hold fast, not in the hope of making anything better in the world or for myself, but simply because I cannot live without some sort of reverence. . . .

I notice increasingly among younger parents of handicapped children a healthy trend toward creative-movement activities as release. I am reminded of the first question members of the Bantu tribe of Africa ask any stranger, namely, "What do you dance?" The response tells them what they wish to know about the new person. We declare ourselves through our patterns of movement.

Mrs. Travis, the young mother of a child with Down's syndrome, told me how she utilized creative dance whenever she needed to express herself freely, to open up and let go. She had gotten the idea from Laura Archer Huxley's marvelous book on self-enlightenment and improvement, *You Are Not The Target*. When feeling trapped, inhibited, down-hearted, or "over-requested" she would, at the first opportunity, go into a room by herself, turn on a favorite piece of music, remove all of her clothes, and dance. Yes, remove all her clothes and dance! Release all her inhibitions! No judgments of one's appearance or movements. Freedom is the goal—freedom physically, emotionally. Dancing for no eyes, only for your feelings, especially those not easily expressed. Dancing the feelings you cannot ordinarily express to anyone, perhaps not even to yourself. The throwing off of clothes encourages the tossing away, of fears, embarrassments, compulsions, social sensitivities. The idea is to be yourself fully, unmasked. And whatever you most deeply feel, let that feeling become the dance. Feel every atom of the frustration, fear, desire, or joy. Dance the feelings out into the open. Let them engulf you. Open! Dare! Open!

There is little joy in being closed, closed off, cut off, in prison. Many years ago, a wise physician, Walter B. Cannon, wrote a simple but profound little book entitled *The Wisdom of the Body*. The body, being wise, outfoxes the mind, dances and revels if given half a chance, not out of need for mere physical activity but for joy, that wonderful energy which is in excess of the level required for simply keeping alive. Here again, the ancients, as in all of life's fundamental wisdoms, point out the way for us:

Cease, Man, to mourn, to weep, to wail;
  enjoy the shining hour of sun;
We dance along Death's icy brink,
  but is the dance less full of fun?

The Kasidah

There are many basic truths in human existence; in one sense, living is the search for these truths. To open oneself can be wonderful; but to open is to disclose, to reveal, to un-cover—here lies the risk, the possibility of having our open-ness responded to painfully. Each of us improves the human condition to the extent that we do not interfere with the paths others take to be happy, even though they seem odd, to the extent that we are not unkind to others. None of us has full insight into all of life's ideals or ways of being human.

We need to realize this basic truth: None of us is a fixed entity, but a living, seeking, dynamic being with potential for discovery, change, and creative relationships. To realize our potential as mother, as father, as child, or as workers, we must live not to feel constantly safe, but with the courage to meet insecurity, not with panic or fright, but with some positive sense of risk that can precede moments of discovery, and even of joy.

Isn't it strange how the most important things seldom get done, while the most trivial things (doing the dishes, emptying the wastebasket, eating on time) always get done? And yet, as the Zen master said, "To become accustomed to anything is a terrible thing."

14
ENJOYING

Enjoy yourself. It's
later than you think.

Old Saying

131

A famous poet, visiting Italy, walked along a street filled with many beggars. One was attracting more attention and receiving more donations than the others. The poet approached him and discovered why; the man was wearing a sign that said: "It is April, and I am blind."

Too often we forget to remember all of the happy and beautiful things which surround us. We forget to respond to our need to be gay, to feed the spirit—instead, we dampen these callings with endless small distractions or with too much emphasis on the burdens we bear. We fail to nourish our appetites for beauty and serenity. As I think of these matters in relation to parents of handicapped children, a pleasant memory comes to mind:

The Miller home, from the outside, appeared quite humble, surrounded by run-down industrial buildings. Mrs. Miller escorted me through the plain, clean living room, but as I reached the entrance to Billy's room, I was surprised by its beauty. The thirteen-year-old turned his wheelchair toward me as I stepped inside. He spoke in a labored, drawn-out monotone, "Good morning." I returned the greeting, adding, "What a beautiful room this is! It looks like a Japanese teahouse." Mrs. Miller seemed pleased to explain: "My father was a World War II veteran. He spent some time in Japan after the war. He brought home a few things from there, including those two vases you see, and he told me many times about the Japanese tea ceremony. I loved the story and never forgot it. A few years ago, I realized that Billy's cerebral palsy would always keep him—and me—in the house a lot of the time. This is the biggest room we have, and I decided to set it up as Billy's—but it's ours, really—and to do it in the Japanese style. I read several books from the library. I wanted a place we spent so much time in to be nice looking."

How well she had succeeded! The room was almost severely plain, but with well-proportioned materials obviously chosen carefully. Crossing the white ceiling were wooden beams, their deep brown wood smooth and rich-looking. The rice wallpaper suggested the paper walls of Japan. There were two windows, one large and one small, both louvered. "They are almost always open," Mrs. Miller explained, "to let in the sounds—not just the machinery and truck noises, but the sounds of birds or people's voices. A house should be a shelter, but it shouldn't shut out the world." The walls were bare except for a hanging Japanese scroll—a delicate painting of a mountain forest and stream. On the bookshelf stood a lovely dry-flower arrangement of hydrangeas and orange chrysanthemums.

Just outside, the tiny yard contained a small plum tree and a small azalea bush. A soft rain fell. We chatted for a while, then sipped our tea together in silence, noting, it seemed to me, with respect and appreciation the beauty of these simple things.

Mrs. Miller broke the silence. "We may not be rich, and it's hard to make things go right sometimes, what with the hospital and the schools and, oh, the transportation headaches. But that doesn't mean we can't have some peace and beauty in our lives." Before I left, I asked, "Why a plum tree?" "I had thought of pine," she replied. "Pine is for long life, they say, but the plum stands for courage. I learned that in my reading. You see,. the plum sends out its blossoms while there is still snow on the ground."

How complicated we so often make our lives. "Simplify, simplify, simplify," said Thoreau. We must learn to see below the surface and into the essence of things—to see what truly matters, that life with moments of beauty in it is certainly a better life.

I also recall a quite different home. The mother of a little girl dying of cancer obviously liked trinkets. The house seemed filled with what appeared to be inexpensive perfume bottles, costume jewelry, and various other articles of popular fashion—rings of little monetary value, stuffed animals from a nearby amusement park, five-and-dime store dolls, plastic flowers, paint-by-numbers pictures, Hollywood movie magazines, and scores of kitchen knickknacks. But Anne and her mother had a loving and mutually nourishing relationship. In time, they helped me to realize that such baubles were not mere trifles. The beaded handbag was not merely a carrying-case; it was a symbol representing one day's shopping adventure. Those flowers of plastic were not merely flowers. All were the symbols and the substance of love, of magic shared, of companionship, of lively conversations over purchases. These simple things served love and relationship. They were associated with fun and liveliness where gloom and non-life threatened. They were messengers, I thought, instruments with which to do battle with the world, battle cries, the sound of trumpets!

I am always surprised in my university graduate courses when I ask the students, most of whom have years of experience working with parents of handicapped children, if they can recall sharing a funny experience or having a truly enjoyable laugh together with parents in connection with their handicapped children. Fewer than ten percent are able to recall such a moment, and that to me has always seemed remarkable. When I ask why this is so, I get many answers, all logical: "We are dealing with serious problems." "We have to concentrate on the problems." "It is no laughing matter." Closer to the truth, perhaps, is the reality that as clinicians we try to present some image of perfection concerning our professional role, while as parents we become trapped in the sin of seriousness, which only joy can redeem. Imagine two people being together for one to five hours per week over a period of a year or two—a total of several hundred hours, and not one moment of laughter!

It is as though we were saying, "The joy of the present and the future must be diminished by the sadness and seriousness of what has happened." Must it be so? All of the animals except man, Samuel Butler once said, know that the principle business of life is to enjoy it. The eminent philosopher, Alfred North Whitehead, felt that the purpose of existence is to live, to live well, to live better.

In one meeting with a panel of parents, it was eye-opening to observe the difference in reactions to the question, "Do parents of handicapped children have any rights?" "Parents' rights?" pondered one mother. "I suppose we must have some, but I can't think of any." "What a laugh!" said another. "It's high time somebody talked about those. All I've heard since halfway through the pregnancy is my responsibilities!" But others expressed their belief in their own rights. Parents have a right, they stated, "to some time to themselves in the evening," "to see a television program of their own choosing once in a while," "to read a paper in peace," "to have a desk or place that's out-of-bounds to their youngsters," "to have some fun on their own sometimes," "to be cranky when they feel cranky," "to tell the kids off when they're impossible," "to expect some cooperation from the family." The list could go on forever—and even though "rights" sometimes amount to "gripes," the "gripes" are understandable.

Beverly Sills, the great and gracious opera singer and mother of two severely impaired children, seems always to be gay-spirited, an "up" person. Directly to the point, Miss Sills says, "Sad people are boring." It's true! Boredom is one of life's worst enemies. And overconcerned attention to everyday tasks can muffle the joy of existence. "I go about my chores like a sad washerwoman," said one mother. "I'm like a robot, I lose all sense of meaning. I get no pleasure out of life." And of course, professional workers locked into fixed habit patterns are qualified to make a similarly woeful declaration.

To Maurice Friedman, esteemed scholar of Hasidism, the most painful Hasidic saying is this: "A human being who has not a single hour for his own every day is not a human being." We, ourselves, frequently choose our own forms of slavery. Too often we count only the bad experiences, forgetting that one good experience is worth ten bad ones.

"When do you know or feel that you are really *enjoying* life?" I asked a large group of parents. They replied with words that described or were associated with their feelings of joy: *happiness, delight, glad, awe, a sense of mystery, humble gratitude, alive and positive, open, healthy, radiant, keenly aware of all things, sexy, loving, fully giving and receiving, all-of-a-piece, together, beautiful, in a state of harmony, loss of conscious, awareness of myself, up, high, liberated, free.* Just saying, writing, or thinking such words seems to provide an emotional lift. And these parents had definite ideas of what "enjoying" was *not*: It was *not* self-pity, doubt, or guilt; or feeling trapped or feeling embarrassed; it was *not* a self-conscious and determined pursuit of commercial pleasure; it was *nothing* unkind. The responses to what constitutes joy are limitless once we go with the flow of being fully alive, of revitalizing ourselves. As one worker said, "It's when I'm creating something; when I'm helping others to be happier; when I feel necessary to the life of another. I find myself appreciating little things—the smell of cranberries cooking, fresh air, a wrinkled face, a maple leaf."

One of the delights of my life as a counselor occurred the day a formerly chronically depressed mother of a schizophrenic boy began our session by declaring, "Today, I don't want to talk about problems. I want to talk about all the good things in my life." Halleluljah! We spent the hour talking of these high points, but mostly about her gardening. In her world of tensions she could get down on her knees in good soil and know that her hands were in Earth's basic resource; there, in her often complicated world, she was in contact with something essentially unchanging, simple, and fundamental. There, at the end of day, in her garden she could listen to the evening songs of birds, see good plants come from the seeds she had planted. The spirit craves contact with the simple truths. The mind needs to know that certain things endure and grow; work in the furrow can get one out of life's rut.

For many years I have asked parents, "What idea has been most helpful to you in terms of enjoying life?" I remember several responses: "I look for the possible good, and go after it." "I become more content when I remind myself that to be happy doesn't require *complete* happiness. Even Babe Ruth struck out over a thousand times." "I try to live the happy life I know is within me." "I make the most of the possibilities." One parent said, "I let myself act like a little kid once in a while— rolled down a hill the other day!" The father of a hyperactive nine-year-old admitted that he and his wife had not only learned to go on occasional weekends together away from the responsibilities of the family and home, but from time to time each went off alone for a day or two. Devotion is admirable, but overdevotion is unwise. It is a terrible thing to live *entirely* for and through others.

I have asked some groups of parents to write down words referring to laughing: *smile, grin, guffaw, chuckle, giggle, snicker, burst out laughing, roar.* Almost without fail, the mood of the group becomes happier after such an exercise. It's difficult to stay grim when you're smiling, and it's difficult even when you're just *thinking* about smiling or laughing. One parent brought in a notebook she shared with the group; it was filled with pictures she had cut out from newspapers and magazines, each one showing a person laughing uproariously. No one who looked at this book ever failed to laugh. A father donated a sign to our clinic which said: "Keep smiling, and you'll worry the hell out of people." I made another sign with some words by Thackery: "The world is a looking glass and gives back to everyone the reflection of his own face."

One mother of a brain-injured, hyperactive boy had to learn to laugh again, as she recalled in a letter to me:

Many times I was at the end of my rope. He was always go, go, going, like a bull in a china shop. There were so many years of constantly being on the watch, fears of his hurting himself—or others, being on the alert for any accidents, and battling with him, actually, and *never* being able to breath a sigh of relief, to just relax. I knew I was ready to throw in the towel when I suddenly realized I'd almost lost my sense of humor. In my quiet moments—usually late at night—I had a chance to—to meditate, I guess, to take a look at my life and my relationships with people. I needed to figure out how to live more happily. It took some effort to change. But I decided that enjoying, that laughing, was the key, and I watched for the funny moments. I began finding them.

Moments of calm solitude and of laughter deepen our sense of the wonder, goodness, and mystery of life. Time is short, and we must find the most meaningful and joyous paths. Flowers lose their bloom, and leaves fade; we, too, bloom and fade. Each moment should be as relished as a lovely flower.

Stuart Chase, eminent teacher and semanticist, almost sixty years ago wrote of those times in which he felt truly alive. He included those moments when he was creating something; those times when he could be in view of the sea, mountains, or stars; moments of loving; moments of conversation, exchanging ideas with good friends; when in the presence of some danger—such as rock-climbing; moments of *play*; taking food when genuinely hungry; drinking water from a cool mountain spring after a hard climb. Not least, he added, "I live when I *laugh*—spontaneously and heartily." The mother of a retarded girl recently said this to me:

No longer do I do only what I'm supposed to do, what people *expect* me to do, what I *ought* to do. Now and then, now, I do what I really *want* to do. I believe what I want to believe.

This mother had learned that she felt better when she was happy, and that other people gravitated toward individuals who laughed or were happy—people who could laugh at themselves and with others. Deep in our hearts lies a knowledge that times of laughter are times remembered; that action done with humor is usually done well; that one does not sin when happy, does no evil when happy, wrongs no creature, including self. Inside each breast lies the knowledge that laughter loosens up, opens up, frees; as the old maxim goes, a little nonsense now and then is relished by the wisest men. "All the Constitution guarantees," said Ben Franklin, "is the pursuit of happiness. You have to catch up with it yourself."

I remember one vivacious mother saying to me, "I do my best work without killing myself, and I have fun—much, much fun." Another gave this advice: "Don't react to every single crisis—every fifth or tenth perhaps. All those telephone calls back, appointments to be made, letters to answer, things to shop for. I learned that nothing of any real importance gets accomplished if we react to every crisis." Another said simply, "My life is as frustrating as ever, but now I'm more humorously resigned to it."

One morning, feeling that our group of mothers of pre-school children with severe learning disabilities had a need for a moment of levity, I began the meeting by giving each of the six ladies a small card and said, "Because we have been talking so seriously about being tense and anxious, I'd like to get your reactions to the suggestions made by Satchel Paige, the great baseball pitcher. I've put a different one of his suggestions on each card. Let's each read ours aloud in turn and see what the group thinks about them. The result was one of the liveliest, most pleasant, and helpful sessions we ever had. Here are Satchel's well-known recommendations for enjoying life:

1. Avoid fried meat which angry up the blood.
2. If your stomach disputes you, lie down and pacify it with cool thoughts.
3. Keep your juices flowing by jangling around gently as you move.
4. Go very light on vices such as carrying on in society. The social ramble ain't restful.
5. Avoid running at all times.
6. Don't look back. Something may be gaining on you!

"Before we can bring happiness to others," Maurice Maeterlinck observed almost a century ago, "we first must be happy ourselves; nor will happiness abide within us unless we confer it upon others." Joy is wise. And the little joys are usually the most enduring. Happiness linked to the possessive instinct is of lesser value—things acquired matter less than experiences shared. Remember, things possessed are ours only on loan—the land we live on, the table at which we sit—ours only for a time. Erich Maria Remarque, in his novel *Flotsam,* has one of his characters ask why one should want to have possessions when we do not even own our existence; it is slipping away from us every second. Thus, the wisdom and necessity of never neglecting the little joys.

It is strange, in a sense, how things become more unattainable the more desperately we seek them. The bird of paradise really does not alight on the grasping hand. An attitude or mood of quiet openness to the possibilities of joy is a wiser way, suggested in an ancient Japanese Koan, which I recall in this form:

> Sitting quietly
> Doing nothing,
> Spring comes
> And the grass grows by itself.

Let's admit it. There are some among us who take life too damned seriously. Perhaps Abe Lincoln was right when he noted that folks are about as happy as they make up their minds to be. Some believe that it is not possible to learn in laughter as well as in tears of fears. Joy and seriousness—we see the two extremes of emotions depicted in Nikos Kazantzakis's *Zorba The Greek*. To Zorba, to be a person means to be free—free to play his stringed santuri when the spirit moved him. To his boss, it means freedom from real attachment to another. The boss, accepting everything as fate, is incapable of either grief or anger. He has fallen so low that if he had to choose between falling in love with a woman and reading a book about falling in love, he would choose the book. Zorba sees each day in its pure freshness; to him every bird, tree, or cloud is a miracle.

"For to miss the joy is to miss all," said Robert Louis Stevenson, ". . . the personal poetry, the enchanted atmosphere, that rainbow work of fancy that clothes what is naked and seems to enoble what is base, . . . (no person) lives in the external truth among salts and acids, but in the warm, phantasmagoric chamber of his brain, with the painted windows and the storied wall."

But what if we feel guilty about enjoying ourselves? Many parents know this feeling. "I get a sense of shame," said one parent, "which comes whenever I feel better." Some feel guilt if they even *anticipate* or daydream of a happier situation, as though to say, "I do not deserve to be thus favored." Guilt is an extremely undesirable and usually undeserved emotion. Yet it can be ever-present, overpowering: "It interferes with all my pleasures." "I cannot forgive myself for . . ." One parent spoke of her double trap: "Knowing that guilt is an undesirable feeling, I also then feel guilty about feeling guilty."

But it is our opportunity and perhaps our obligation to go beyond guilt, to a larger view of future possibilities, to a refreshed appreciation of the present and a renewed respect for our own worthiness. Parents know about care and sorrow, but they owe themselves and one another the will to discover the bright shafts of delight amid the dark clouds of circumstance.

Yes, perhaps it is an obligation to go beyond guilt, to say together, "We are obliged—to enjoy!" Of course, there may be times when guilt may stop us, and the reactions of neighbors may, also. But if we do not enjoy, we become a burden to all, even to our children, who may feel guilty for depriving us of good times. But the more we enjoy life, the more others enjoy us, derive happiness from us.

Certainly, it's ridiculous to assume that we must or can be happy at all times. Sometimes it is simply impossible not to feel miserable:

My friends try to wave it all away. If only one of them would cry with me just once.

It truly is an awesome burden to try to have nothing but nice feelings.

Oh, I'm feeling low a lot, but when I'm with another parent who is depressed, I try to cheer her up. I might ask, "What's the nicest thing that's happened to you this week?" and, you know, just trying to remember a happy moment seems to improve the mood. Then I feel better. Oh, for myself—I have my daydreams, my little fantasies—little pleasures that don't harm anybody.

The well-known historian, Will Durant, once told of his search for happiness: first, in knowledge, which merely caused disillusionment; then in travel, finding only weariness; in wealth, finding only irritability and worry; then, in writing, finding only fatigue. One day he observed a man getting off a train, walking over to a car in which sat a woman holding her sleeping infant. The man kissed the woman and more gently kissed the baby so as not to waken it. The family then drove off, leaving Durant with a discovery about real happiness, that life's normal, common functions hold the possibility of some delight.

It is an old maxim that the secret of happiness is something to do, something to love, and something to hope for. All parents hold access to this secret. The mere attempt to enjoy life to the fullest increases happiness. Happiness, in turn, improves the capacity to see the beautiful; only love does it better, although love and happiness are special forms of each other. It is not always easy to enjoy. There is a courage of happiness, Maeterlinck believed, as real as the courage of sorrow.

In closing this section, may I leave with you these words of Goethe, words I have had posted in my clinic office for many years:

. . . **one ought every day at least, to hear a little song, read a good poem, see a fine picture and, if it were possible, to speak a few reasonable words.**

Nothing stands still.
Nothing has, nothing will.

A.T.M.

LEARNING

In the Prado museum in Madrid there is a drawing by Goya of an old man hobbling along on two sticks. Written below are these words: *Aun apprendo* ("I am still learning"). In being with special children, one could hardly say otherwise as parent or as worker.

We can learn much of life from special children. Being handicapped may be thought of as a dramatic instance of the human condition: Each of us has been a little deaf, a little blind, a little slow to respond, emotionally off-center, even speechless. We have been sometimes at least a little fearful, angry, confused, or physically awkward. We have sensed in at least a small way what handicapped means—and some of us, indeed, perhaps have truly qualified as impaired, at least for a time. Living or working long hours with a severely handicapped individual is sometimes like watching grand theatre; great drama emanates from some universal human condition or experience that touches and is given off by us all. Each of us can identify with the absurdity in the situation of a brilliant young man who cannot communicate his brilliance normally because he is unable to speak or write without a struggle—he has cerebral palsy. We can empathize with the sorrow of parents whose son, brain-injured in a motorcycle accident, is now severely paralyzed. We respond in recognition to the joy of other parents whose child has suddenly, at age ten, learned how to read. Perhaps we might not experience the essential anguish, compassion, doubt, or delight, but the varied limits of

146

human existence are at least suggested to us. These lessons special children may teach.

What is required in both parent and child for significant learning to occur? Thousands of books have been written on the learning process and the "laws of learning." What is usually omitted in these volumes turns out to be that which is most crucial in the learning experiences or transactions of parents and their children. What constitutes cruciality? I suggest that degrees and forms of hope, faith, love, trust, and courage do. The learning of fundamental skills and techniques is very important, it cannot be denied. But the fundamental purpose of all education—including special education—is not simply to improve specific abilities; it should also be to help us bring meaning to our lives, to appreciate beauty, graciousness, and kindness and, in a larger degree, to appreciate the past, to be most fully aware of the present, to be courageous toward what is to come.

As a clinician working with a broad spectrum of human impairments, one learns much and constantly from the children and families one meets. One learns, for instance, that regardless of labels of groups of children, no two children are alike; each must be approached in terms of his or her particularity. One learns that the most important "diagnostician" may be the child or parents—what they believe to be the case is often the reality that suggests the professional focus. One also learns that educational or therapy structures are available along a broad continuum—the needs of special children and their families vary so enormously that it is presumptuous to assume that any one approach is suitable for most, much less all. And one learns that children and parents can and should contribute actively to the professional program.

Perhaps one of the most basic lessons workers with families having special needs have learned is this: The personal qualities of clinicians and clients are frequently much more important than the materials or methods used. Many philosophers, writers, clinicians, and educators have long recognized that an accurate and sensitive awareness of another person's feelings, a deep concern for the other person's welfare without efforts to dominate, and an open, nondefensive genuineness will benefit any human interaction. Humanistic psychologists have stressed the importance of various characteristics of counselors; a good counselor should:

1. Be trustworthy, dependable, or consistent in some deeply important sense.
2. Be able to express attitudes of interest, respect, liking, and caring.
3. Perceive the client as wanting to grow and as capable of contributing importantly to his own improvement.
4. Think, feel, and speak "all-of-a-piece"—thoughts, feelings, and words match.
5. Be in tune with his or her own feelings and be able to express them spontaneously but with no need to satisfy personal motivations that interfere with client progress.
6. View the client as capable not only of being fully in the present in accord with his or her abilities, but as capable of growing.

Perhaps one could say more simply that, to fulfill their therapeutic functions, workers in the human services must be persons of deeply felt sympathy who have a genuine and persistent desire to be of help. Might not all of these characteristics be considered desirable in *any* interpersonal relationship? In terms of special education, for example, may we not ask: What is reading—without reverence? What is knowing—without love? What is learning—without heart?

In thinking of those times of asking parents what they have learned—with and about their special child, themselves, the agencies and procedures they have experienced—a variety of recollections occur. For example, parents I have known who believed their relationships with agencies or professionals were successful made statements of the following kind:

They included me in the activity planning right from the start.

She not only did her own job but always tried to keep me informed of all the other services and agencies we'd be needing. She'd go out of her way—was really concerned.

The clinic shared everything with us—what they knew about Margie, giving us copies of important records, treating us with respect.

She helped me to feel better about my son and about myself without kidding anybody—I mean, she helped us see the limits, too. She helped me to get beyond "whose fault" to "nobody's fault."

I learned that I could really do something, not just hope and wait for others to act.

One comes to learn also that parents as well as children have different learning styles that must be respected. From time to time, for instance, when words are not enough, nonverbal procedures may be brought into play, such as body sculpture in family counseling. Here the counselor asks the "sculptor" (parent or child) to position the other persons in a way that shows some important characteristic about the person or group. Usually we suggest a group sculpture, each member taking a turn in altering the sculpture or creating an original one. Facial expressions may be molded, too. Sculptors may work themselves into the tableau. The counselor intermittently comments or interprets and may speak with the tableau members. One of the great benefits of body sculpture is that it encourages touching. Also, "statements" are often made in this approach which have been difficult to express verbally.

Another variation that has proven helpful is to have members make a declaration in sculpture concerning how they would like to see the group or individual develop in the future.

At times the effect of body sculpture is eye-opening. One deaf adolescent positioned his parents in erect standing positions, heads up and arms held straight down rigidly against their sides, facing away from each other. He then sat down facing away from them, staring out the window. When asked how he would make the sculpture most beautiful, he positioned them all sitting in a circle, facing one another and holding hands. When asked once more to edit it, he changed only his position, standing up as though about to walk away, blowing both parents a kiss with one hand and waving goodbye with the other.

Most parents, I believe, come to realize that life must be lived not through another's misery or one's own, but rather through each other's happiness; life must be lived not by sacrifice, but by one's strengths and the search for joy—therein lies survival and renewal. Sometimes the significant learning revolves around single lessons, such as the following:

It wasn't until we finally realized that his brain-injury was not the cause of all the bad behavior that things began to improve. He was always restless, lots of emotional outbreaks. We got to the point that we really resented it—but we felt guilty, too. So we gave in to him just to have some peace and quiet. Then we realized he was taking advantage of us all the more. Anyway, we thought, the world outside the family wasn't so protected, he'd find it more frustrating, so we started setting limits. As soon as we did that, letting him know very clearly what we expected and what he could expect from us, too, the whole situation improved—for all of us.

And I remember Mr. Luis, who taught me many a lesson:

Hey, intelligence is great—I admire it. Artistic ability is great, too. And sports skills. Being good looking is fine, too. But most people don't have all those things—certainly our kids—my kid doesn't. But do you know what he has that a lot of people don't have? A good sense of humor. He really knows how to laugh—how to enjoy. He's the most generous kid I know. And he's never hurt another soul—he's kind. Why can't we respect all of these great things as much as the other ones?

At such times, workers recognize that they are co-learners in the process of interacting with parents and child, although counselors may not view themselves as teachers in the traditional sense. There are, of course, phases in dealing with children who have special needs when parents may be assisted in ways of observing, recording, or noting behavior, or periods of training in the application of certain procedures, such as reinforcement techniques applied to specific behaviors. Although these may be of great importance to the child's total program, where underlying critical relationships between parents and child are concerned one really cannot *tell* parents how to behave as parents. In such instances, I personally believe I can discuss varieties of ways of being a parent, share my own experiences or those of others, act as a sounding board, but I cannot really tell them exactly how to behave.

In efforts to learn continuingly in order to serve more efficiently, workers who are still growing professionally frequently evaluate their own behavior, as reflected in the following statement:

As a first-year teacher of a class of hyperactive, disturbed children, after particularly difficult days I'd think I had it worse than any of their parents could with them individually. I soon realized that I didn't have to be with these troubled youngsters through every night and weekend and vacation as their parents did. Nor did I even have to take care of things like their parents did when the kids got ill or hurt in some way. And I could always ventilate with the other teachers—some of these parents had no one to turn to. So I'm glad to do what I try to do—help them to grow.

Ask parents of handicapped children or those who work with them what they have learned from special children and they may answer: "patience," "tolerance," "to keep things in perspective," "humility." One mother of five children, two of whom were seriously handicapped, made this statement:

Not only have I learned to take the larger view of things, but I've learned that I can take a lot of pain and yet survive. In a way, I've been allowed to discover the extent of my own strength; that I can not only survive but I can live a full and happy life. Somehow, in working out their problems, I've learned more about myself. Even when things got difficult I found that support of others and my own faith carried me through. I think any parent can experience this, but a child with a special problem heightens the whole awareness. Oh, I've also learned not to be disappointed—not *too* disappointed. And only the other day I realized that, while my older children no longer had, at least with me, their old sense of inquisitiveness—now they seem to know everything—my two slow ones still are inquisitive about everything—they still have a kind of *joie de vivre*—a simple love of living. I realize now that I appreciate that childlike sense they have—it serves a need I have as a mother. I'm not sure I should always feel this way, but I certainly do right now. That's part of what they are for me—through them I seem to see myself more clearly.

Each mind and heart, no matter how weak or hurt, feels frustration, pain, or pleasure—each is human. And each human deserves patience, respect, and humility—these are often the very virtues our special children help us to learn. Just as we discover the strength of our houses from the elements that beset it, we discover our own courage and strength from the fates that challenge us. Caring for—or living life as—a special child can be a special challenge. But it can provide a special opportunity, too—an opportunity to learn about ourselves through a creative relationship with someone who needs us. We may, as unique learners, respond to this opportunity in many ways, but respond we must. There is a Russian proverb that says, "Everyone goes to the forest, but some go for a walk to be inspired, and others go to cut down the trees." Each one of us decides how we will seek out the meanings of life's patterns and mysteries. And we are still learning.

May I dare as I never have done. May I persevere as I have never done. . . . May my melody not be wanting to the season.

Henry David Thoreau, Journals

DARING

A well-known racing car driver was once asked if he did not think it was true that, of all sports, only mountaineering, bullfighting, and automobile racing really tried the participant, and that all the others were only recreations. He agreed. "This is not a game that is basically a game for boys, like baseball," he said. "In this game you must put up a bond for your life every time you go out to play. But because it is a very demanding game it is spiritually very rewarding, too." Camus in *The Rebel* put a similar idea this way: "The maximum danger implied the maximum hope."

In the "game" of being responsible for a handicapped child, one frequently puts up a bond for each major decision or action taken which could affect the life of the child importantly, for better or for worse. Some parents never take a risk, indeed live so as to avoid major decisions, fearful that the wrong one will be made, or that a loss of some kind—love, perhaps—will occur if one invests too much of oneself in the interpersonal relationship. Others, while typically avoiding foolhardiness, from time to time will take the risk of making a passionate investment in an action that may make them appear foolish—or cause them to feel gloriously happy.

Risk-avoiders sometimes find themselves in a paradoxical position that causes them to cling to some concrete reality, even a painful one, in order to avoid the unbearable stress of what is *possible*: the mother of a severely handicapped child who could not bring herself to reveal to her husband, for fear of losing his love, that she wanted to place their child in a residence outside their home; the father who could not find a way to tell his son, who had struggled with a learning disability but now was succeeding academically, that he loved him very much and always had; the parents of a bright, cerebral-palsied young man who could not allow him to begin traveling about the city independently even though he and others who knew him believed he could do so, and that he would grow in the process. Such parents sometimes are those who have difficulty fully expressing and sharing their deeper feelings in any person-to-person situation. As one parent remarked, "I never get close enough to life to realize what I have left out."

The courage to dare, to take the risk of a passionate investment—in expressing one's deeper nature, in revealing oneself to another—may, of course, be hard-pressed within the special child or youth, too, far more than we realize. A student who had continued to stutter severely throughout his high-school years, and who had been trying desperately to muster up courage to speak to a young lady he much admired, was scared to death he'd make a complete fool of himself. He came into my office one day, beaming:

I finally let myself go with this girl. I mean I was just myself, stuttering too. It wasn't easy. But she didn't seem to act any differently so I just went on. We took a walk. It was raining. But everything was soft and quiet and warm. And I spoke to her of how it made me feel. I said that feelings were the most important thing, even sad, melancholy ones. And I said maybe these feelings were a block to my getting along with others. She didn't think so at all. I told her about feelings I couldn't even tell my parents or friends. Perhaps I can be this way with others. It felt good, a fine experience. Forgetting everything, even myself, but I was really myself, the person I know I am down deep. Could I be this way with my parents too? Maybe . . . maybe I could.

It *is* possible to grow out of pain, to use hurting circumstances in creative ways, but it requires encouragement, persistence, faith. There are those parents who have shared their trials and triumphs freely with others in similar circumstances; those who have written books or articles telling their stories as parents of handicapped children; handicapped persons, themselves, who have written compelling autobiographies—one need only think of Helen Keller, whose writings are aglow with courage, insight, and beauty. Yes, sweet can be the uses of adversity. But adversity can also be sour, or at least difficult, as these cases indicate:

Look, you probably think I'm too protective of my son, but who knows him better than we do? He got into a bus last summer and got lost. The bus driver called a policeman and they tossed him into jail—drunk and disorderly conduct, they charged. They didn't let him make a phone call for twelve hours, believe it or not! So he has this brain-injury—ataxia—you know, he stumbles around, and his speech is, well, we can understand him but most people can't. We found out he was just trying to get directions. He got excited and a lady got frightened. The judge dismissed the case—he knew what it was. But he said we had to give him more supervision. Now, is that *overprotection?*

My David is very expressive. He expresses his feelings in the open. But once he touched a girl's hair and we had trouble. He can do this with his sisters, but he hasn't learned the difference yet between sisters and other girls. Trouble is, he tries so hard to do the right thing. *He* always has to make the adjustment, not others. If he tries his hardest and does well, nobody gives him any credit because then he just looks normal. But if he gets upset, makes a scene, everybody jumps on him. How are you supposed to know when to encourage him to do something on his own, or when to put the brakes on? It's hard to make those decisions. You're afraid you'll make the wrong ones. Sometimes, believe me, it takes courage *not* to do something—just stand there and hope for the best. That's hard to do, too!

The entire dependency-independency issue is a major one for parents and children. Do we leave him in the care of a baby sitter? What will happen if there's an emergency? Will she remember to take him to the toilet on time? Will she understand what he's saying? The questions and doubts are endless. They are not significantly different questions from those we ask about typical children, but a special condition somehow casts them in a slightly more ominous light, whatever the child's age.

My son's birth-injury left him with poor coordination, as you know. I nearly fainted when a neighbor came to the door carrying Karl. He had blood all over his face and hands. I should never have gotten that bike, I thought. This was the third time in two days he'd had a bike accident. But, yet, after I found that the cuts were superficial and I calmed down, I realized my reactions were really about the same as I'd have for my other boys. There'd be no going ahead for Karl if he didn't find out what he could really do. Yet it's difficult to go ahead on these things when so many people are saying you shouldn't. So there is a risk—for everybody. As your speech therapist said, "Sometimes kids grow up not because of us, but in spite of us."

The ideal relationship of parents and child would be continuously and mutually progressive. One of our chief aims should be to liberate any child to the maximum as an individual; then the child can most fully follow his or her *own* path, whether or not that path is the very one *we* might have selected. The child's union with parents should be sealed basically with mature love, strengthened increasingly by comradeship and understanding. In a certain larger sense, perhaps we cannot truly choose precise pathways for our children. We can try to chart our own way clearly and wisely and then use the clarity of that vision to help our children along their own ways. Every decision to act is a risk—but so, also, is every decision *not* to act!

To dare to behave as we believe is something we all have a chance to do—or not do. We have mentioned repeatedly that workers, like parents, must sometimes risk, too. I once wrote in a piece on retarded children that a poem is never completed, it is only abandoned; similarly, the impaired individual must never be abandoned. In clinical endeavors, we cannot always defer action until a scientific demonstration is provided. Since we always need to go on in life, we must take risks in accordance with intuitions or solutions that are neither ridiculous nor logically certain, but only probable. Where we are unable to prove, we believe; where we cannot demonstrate, we make a choice. To the degree that we follow this guide, to that degree do we dare, dare to risk for the sake of a larger good, with the courage to accept the consequences if we fail.

It is commonly recognized that any learning in counseling which involves a change in self-organization, in the way one regards oneself and behaves, tends to be threatening and will often be resisted. This threat—this risk—holds as true for special children as it does for parents or workers. I want to mention again how similar are the challenges and pitfalls experienced by parents and workers. Among teachers, therapists, and clinicians, for instance, it is often easier simply to focus on more obvious or manageable behavior over which we can perhaps feel a sense of control and, therefore, comfort; this is true whether the behavior selected is an apparently simple difficulty (such as the substitution of one speech sound for the appropriate one, a problem in linking a spoken sound with the appropriate letter, reversals in writing) or any simple, easily understood technique for dealing with such behaviors. It is simpler to focus on the obvious, but not necessarily wise, or even sufficiently helpful. The need to know precisely what we are doing, reflected in fixed ideas or techniques, can constitute a danger if it leads to suspicion of innovation or creative thought. Alfred North Whitehead might have termed such the "fallacy of misplaced concreteness." In addition to technique, however, we need to develop a greater tolerance for and sense of *the possible*—in terms of techniques, of what we think children can become—of what we think parents and children in relationship can become and of what children themselves think they can become.

And just as parents need to keep a close watch on their own motives so, too, do workers—again, this is something workers and parents share. Let me cite a personal example: A colleague refers a client to me. After several weeks of consultation, I realize that there is no movement in our relationship. Upon self-analysis, I realize that I am being too concerned with being successful—I want to prove myself worthy of the confidence my colleague has shown in me. Because I value her, I value her view of me, and I do not wish to disappoint her. I discuss this with the client, and things improve from that point. I recognize a degree of risk in my sharing this observation with my client, but, in this instance at least, the risk turns out well.

But there are those children and adults for whom an open, honest expression of feeling or thought is frightening. They have, in some tortuous way, lost the ability to summon up passion in a moment of giving. They have become afraid of a chilling response from others which would make their overture seem inappropriate, leaving them comical and exposed. And sometimes they grow old, not having lived, mimicking the young yet never hearing life's real music, never participating fully in the dance of life. I am reminded of two dear friends, husband and wife, both very severely impaired with cerebral palsy. I recall the question they put to themselves two decades ago: Shall we have a child? They did. She became a ballet dancer. Literally and figuratively, they *partake* of the dances of life!

One deeply caring parent, Nat Mills, demonstrated his

ability to give openly in an article written for *The Exceptional Parent* magazine. In "Our Daughter's Happiness Depends Upon Her Being Sterile," Mr. Mills wrote poignantly of his fourteen-year-old daughter, who had Down's syndrome; she had dreamed of having a husband and children to love and care for. Her parents believed that her child-bearing capacity would represent for the next thirty-five years a hazard that could impair their daughter's emotional and domestic stability. They welcomed her emerging sexuality as a vital step toward mature adulthood, but decided that her ability to have children had to be destroyed. Mr. Mills' discussion of pregnancy by accident, birth control considerations, paternal abandonment, and sublimated motherhood is a powerful one in which he concluded that no abstract right could or should be allowed to open the gates to abject misery. While others would disagree with this point of view, it does represent the kind of challenge and courage of conviction that many parents of children and youths with special needs experience.

In exceptional lives and in typical ones there are endless opportunities to test one's mettle—to work through doubt into decision—to realize in some part the risk, but to imagine also the possibilities.

I'm afraid, but there's nothing to match my wife's fear of having another child who could be terminal. She really fears for us, but mostly for the possibility of inflicting another injustice on a little baby—a broken life—a life too difficult and too short.

So spoke this father who had never been able to enjoy small children. After the death of his infant son, he had come to feel very close to the departed child, and to other children, which rather surprised him. Misfortune in this instance had brought a greater richness, not only in terms of love and appreciation of children but of persons of any age—ill, weak, or strong.

There is also the courage or daring that occurs when a parent feels the need to break away from daily routine, child and family care, or everyday obligations. Television, for example, can constitute one escape route, but only for a while and only to a limited degree. Once Anne Morrow Lindbergh, commenting on television-watching, said that even daydreaming was more creative; daydreaming at least demanded something of oneself and it fed the inner self. But the wish to break away more fully from the constraints of everyday for many parents remains only a wish, an unfulfilled daydream. Others, recognizing their need to achieve distance from their daily routines, make the decision to *escape,* and in their escape find once more the energy to return to fight the world again. A shopping trip, lunch with an old friend, a visit to a museum exhibit or movie, a day or weekend away with one's mate, a lark of whatever kind—each can restore, renew.

When I'm away from them, in a strange way I'm close to them. The physical separation or isolation doesn't pull us apart— spiritual isolation does. If I don't escape every so often—and for me that means going off someplace quiet, alone—I get resentful, irritable. I now watch for signs that I need relief—short temper, general feeling of unhappiness—and I'm learning to avoid the guilt feelings of leaving the children and my husband. I think this calls for greater maturity on my part, but these times need respect and support from the other family members— without that it doesn't work as well.

The claims of other people frequently limit the activities of parents, and rare are those parents who know no need occasionally to find retreat or solitude. The decision to move toward fresh perspective is reflected in an incident involving author G. K. Chesterton, who lived in a section of London called Battersea. He was packing for a vacation when a friend asked him his destination. Chesterton replied, "Battersea." The friend, puzzled, replied that, since he now lived in Battersea, the intent of his response eluded him. "I am going to Battersea," said Chesterton, "via Paris, Heidelberg, Frankfurt. I am going to wander all over the world until once more I find Battersea. I cannot see any Battersea here, because a cloud of sleep and custom has come across my eyes. The only way to go to Battersea is to go away from it."

Sometimes the only way to see a family, a relationship, a child, or a job is to go away from it for a time. One of the finest writings on the subject of woman escaping is Anne Morrow Lindbergh's *Gift from the Sea,* which the reader may by now recognize as one of my favorite books. In this beautifully written work—the mere reading of which constitutes a sweet and refreshing escape—she spoke for many when she stated that she needed to simplify her life. Yet she recognized that she could not simply leave her responsibilities, that total withdrawal was not possible or even desirable. She realized that she was able to be an island "alone unto herself" only sometimes. Each day needs a period, some point that is a lull in the daily occupations, a space in which nothing happens that demands active participation. There is something deep that hungers for the still moment, the need to "evolve another rhythm" with more creative sessions in it; to sit or lie or walk quietly, empty, bare, open—open to the gifts a different rhythm can bring.

Each of us has our own escape routes if we but remind ourselves of them, and dare to use them. One mother of six children, one of whom was deaf and another mentally retarded, who herself seemed almost always happily alive, shared her particular escape route with our group one day:

Where I find music, or something resembling music, there I try to linger. Nothing replenishes me so much as music or the feeling of music, the feeling of a good resonance or sympathetic vibration, the feeling of a rhythm and a harmony that I otherwise miss in much of my life.

Another mother said:

Every week or two, I ask myself if I've done something silly—on purpose silly—recently, and if the answer is no, I realize I am getting too trapped—too serious about it all.

Each of us, in the deepest recesses of our beings, from time to time detects a wise inner voice that advises, "Go. Do. Dare. Remember yourself. Respect yourself. Restore yourself. Feel your feelings. Act on your best thoughts. Let yourself go." Truly, we cannot always predict the outcomes of our actions. There are no guaranteed risks. There are few predictable ends in our own lives, in the effects of decisions we make concerning our children. Yet we must go on, making decisions, daring to dream and to do. Perhaps parents are, in this sense, like poets: Robert Frost repeatedly spoke of voyages of discovery, of never having started a poem whose end he knew. Keats maintained that poets do not know what they have to say until they say it.

To dare, to risk, to be courageous—on the grand scale, or in the small matters of everyday life—is to increase the chances of inventing oneself, of growing. Never to dare or to risk allows us to survive, but not to live creatively, with a passion. The greatest dare, of course, is the dare to *be oneself fully.*

Why are you not you? Why am I not I? The answers no doubt have something to do with taking or not taking the risk of passionate investments in our own lives, in our relationships with others. But from time to time, when such risks of being oneself fully are taken, creative moments result. Of course it is true that, as the naturalist John Burroughs observed, "We cannot walk through life on mountain peaks. There are rivers and valleys, too." One parent with whom I had shared this observation brought me the following note by the popular writer, Kathleen Norris: "Life is easier to take then you'd think;

all that is necessary is to accept the impossible, to do without the indispensable, and bear the intolerable." We both smiled.

At the outset of this chapter, I referred to automobile racing. Many of today's greatest drivers are sensitive and articulate individuals who demonstrate a peculiarly acute awareness of life, an obvious determination to taste life to the fullest, whether in excitement, love, driving expertise, whatever. There are parents like that; I have met them—unusually capable and integrated individuals who live lives with their handicapped children to the fullest. Their roads also twist and turn, and mastery of their relationships with their children and each other can be terribly perilous. As in the killing of a bull, or a rappel down a sheer mountain wall, auto racing for the highest prizes may occasionally allow for one major error, but seldom two. It is a sport, one observer has said, at which one gets better and better until one gets killed—an exaggeration, perhaps, but not a wild one. On the racing course we find truth in the maxim: "Only those who are willing to give up life know what it is worth." In the course of raising a family with a special child, perhaps the corollary is that only those willing to sacrifice life know what it is worth. Maybe Jack London spoke for many of us when he wrote, "I would rather be ashes than dust."

We can only love what we
know and we can never
know completely what
we do not love.

*Aldous Huxley (The Perennial
Philosophy* [New York: Harper Colophon
Books, 1970], p. 81).

LOVING

The mutually creative ideal we have put forth is the love that places another ahead of oneself, the love that is reflected in wanting to do for another regardless of whether it is something one personally desires. It is the love that C.S. Lewis called "gift-love." It is also the love that makes one vulnerable, as one of my students observed: "When one gives and gives without reference to whether the person is deserving, or likeable, or anything else, you have a vulnerability that is a bit unnerving. After all, they may, in their great trouble, reject your best intentions as unworthy—without any more reason than their acting out of a deep hurt in their lives."

Although it holds true for all of us, a child with special needs requires most specially at least one nurturing relationship with another, one person who cares about him and about whom he cares. Life without at least one such other becomes practically no life at all. In a truly nurturing relationship, at least one of the parties must be in mature touch with self and external reality. One mother who was capable of this mature kind of love made this comment about her retarded son:

I love him as much as my other children, but not necessarily more or less. On some days, at certain times, I suppose I do love him more, but at other times it's less. But that's the way it is with all my children. After all, they're not rocks—they're like moving streams, constantly changing. And what's that expression—you can't step in the same stream twice? Heck, on some days you can't even step in it once! Bless 'em all!

168

To love a thing in the deepest sense is to want it to *live fully,* and to want to live fully oneself in relationship to it. Love may be the key. One of our clinicians was asked how he could stand working day after day with his very active group of developmentally delayed preadolescents. He replied, "I *love* these kids." Upon further questioning, he declared, "Look, I know the facts in their background. I know their abilities. I am up on the knowledge in my field, and I'm pretty well trained. But none of that would be enough unless I really liked them. That keeps me going and, I think, keeps them going too."

Yes, love opens. Love extends patience. Love widens our view of what is possible. It is the case for children and parents. It is also true for workers in the vineyards of the helping professions. Strange that love is such a terribly neglected idea in the education and psychology of special children. It deserves a better fate, for it is fundamental to being human, to learning. Goethe maintained that one did not understand anything unless one loved it, that we are fashioned and shaped by what we love. Thoreau declared that the only way to speak the truth was to speak lovingly. And Carl Jung believed that love put one in a mood to risk everything.

A mother, asked if she weren't sacrificing her life for the sake of her retarded daughter, replied this way:

If I were doing it for the *sake* of sacrifice, if I merely liked the *idea* of sacrifice, rather than liking my daughter for the person she is, I'd agree with you. But this would be self-pity, and I have no need for that. You can sacrifice without harm to yourself or others if you love sufficiently. I can't deny that I may be getting other kinds of satisfaction from it, but the basic feeling I have about it all is one of love. I have no real sense of personal frustration about it.

Where love is denied, where it dies or takes no root at all, then the needs that require love in order to best manifest themselves are left less served or remain unanswered. As Aldous Huxley once observed, bad nurture will starve or smother, will mask or distort the best of natures. And in true love, a mutually creative union—a true symbiotic relationship—develops wherein the one enhances the other without the loss of separate, integrated selves. In neurotic love, the relationship is mutually devouring. Here are two statements—the first by a rebellious high school student, the second by his mother, who was being seen by a different counselor:

Love? That's scarey stuff. It's embarrassing to say you love someone. You can think it, but can you say it? I mean to your own parents? It's like playing poker, isn't it, where you bluff and try to keep the other person from knowing what you're thinking. Then they know your weakness, they know how to play you, you know? They're one up. They've got the advantage on you. No, our family's never been one for showing our feelings—the soft ones I mean. No, I'd as soon die as open up like that.

Oh, I think I could love him—like tell him I love him but, well as somebody here said last week, you could love somebody if you knew exactly what he needs. See what I mean? But how do I know what he needs if he can't tell me—or won't? He ought to be grateful for what we've done—the sacrifices and all that time. But he doesn't care. He's selfish. He needs someone to put the fear of God in him, learn some respect. He ought to be ashamed.

Indeed, loving may be frightening, for to love is also to expose yourself to another. When I express love, I express what is important to me, and, thus, I expose myself to being hurt at just those points at which I am most sensitive. In any case, love can be communicated only if you have it, and you can have it only if you have received it. The great moral of

"Beauty and the Beast" comes to mind: Before one can become lovable, one first has to be loved. Feeling loved, one becomes lovelier—love beautifies.

The Arapesh of New Guinea perhaps have done better. While suckling and caressing the infant, the Arapesh mother places it in contact with other family members, with friends, even with domestic animals, all the while repeating, "Good, good. . . ." Thus, the infant's state of bliss becomes associated with being held securely, fondled, and nursed—with positive links to humans and the rest of life. These beneficial associations become connected with the words accompanying these experiences—words to which the child will, very soon, attach a larger meaning and which, themselves, will carry these healthy associations.

In large measure, we become human to the degree that we have been in loving relationship with others. When I mentioned this recently to a colleague, she was reminded of the characteristic reaching out and touching we often experience with mentally retarded clients. "They reach out for humanness when they reach out to us," she observed. Yet even in those husband-and-wife relationships that apparently have been secure, the presence of a handicapped child has seemed to threaten and occasionally seems to destroy that security. In the latter instances, cracks in the marital foundation probably existed prior to the arrival in the family of the special child. Still, there is no denying that the presence of a child with special needs can place tremendous stress on family relationships, especially those between mates.

My wife used to be eager for me to grow in my work, in any way, but lately she just doesn't seem to care about anything but Jackie. She's incredibly generous and kind, gives of herself a thousand percent, an angel. But she's lost her ability to receive as generously as she gives. I miss her attention, and our sex life isn't what it used to be either.

He's a kid not easy to love. Ever since I can remember he's been a trouble, from his early birth right on. Always hurting himself, breaking things, flunking at school, needing special help. Then he got into drugs, left home two or three times. His only friends were the oddballs—the dropouts, the junkies, the bike-bums—they're all likeable guys, strangely enough, but fringe types. Sam is always a leader with those guys—guess that's why he does it. He's not dumb, but he's a headache. Three bike accidents in the last two years—his knee's no good any more. Listen, he bought a new motorcycle last week, and the first night he had it he left it in our garage with the door open, the steering column unlocked, and the key in the ignition. It was stolen, the first night—a thousand dollars! He's a trial. Still, I love him.

Jim has left it all up to me. All the work, the decisions, the frustrations. Not only is he away more, but when he's around now, he seems to be angrier. Sometimes I think he's ashamed he had a retarded son. But he keeps his feelings to himself more, so I don't know. I just don't know.

Any time a special child and a responsible adult are together represents an attempt at exploring life and making something good of it. And each time we succeed, it constitutes a way of praising life—our lives, the child's. We all are required to have devotion, discipline, some skill, and much patience if our lives are to amount to anything. But to succeed even a little, we also need something we cannot simply train ourselves to acquire—call it luck, and for luck we perhaps can only pray or hope.

Nevertheless, love increases the possibility of success and happiness in the life of and with a child who has special needs. As I think of those parents I have considered most maturely loving, I think they concentrated on nurturing rather than dominating. For them, love was not a win or loss but, rather, a helping and a being helped. And it was often frankly, between themselves, open-heartedly and inoffensively sexy. They knew intuitively that it was possible to speak only the one word "love" and never repeat themselves. A happy few had somehow reached that point where I could imagine each saying to the other, "All the songs I have sung to myself I now feel free to sing to you." Somehow they had come to realize that without love one does not see the full potential of others, may not ever really see them at all.

IMAGINING

18

To see the world in a Grain of Sand,
and a Heaven in a Wild Flower
Hold Infinity in the palm of your hand
And Eternity in an hour.

William Blake, Auguries of Innocence

Many parents wonder what their child might have been under different circumstances. Some parents sorely miss the person their child can never be. And yet, how many parents can say that their children are the fulfillment of their dreams? If they are honest, very few.

I'm interested in the facts, just the facts. I just want to know the results of the current tests and what changes will be made as a result. I'd like to know exactly what you want us to do, and we'll do it. Can you tell us what his behavior will be by the end of the school year? I'd like to know what your goals are and your methods. I know that Tim can make it into the regular class full-time if you just work him harder here. We've got to start him moving if he's going to go on to some college. I'm confident he can be brought up to that level.

This father of a young man with considerable learning difficulty had three other children, all of whom were high achievers. He could not imagine why his son was struggling so; he could not imagine his son's thoughts and feelings; he could not imagine alternate educational programs or goals; he could not imagine a future for his son other than that long ago written down in his book of family expectations. He insisted always on "hard evidence," but had not yet discovered that the beliefs to which he held most firmly concerning his son—those beliefs concerning his son's eventual success in college and the world of work, beliefs held firmly and passionately—were the very beliefs for which there was the least evidence. He could not imagine this to be the case. He simply could not accept his son fully as son-as-he-is; this, too, would have required, at the beginning at least, an act of imagination.

Sometimes imagining contributes to a realistic perspective of what the tomorrows can be. A mother concerned about her retarded son's future, shared her thinking with us:

I'd love to think of him as married, working, having children. But my wish for him is simpler than those things. It's that he has good relationships with other people he likes and who care for him. He is able to be loving, and a long-term relationship of sharing and caring would be nice—it might not necessarily be a sexual one—but it could mean doing things together, looking at a beautiful view or recognizing some of the contentment—and responsibility—that goes with closeness.

In the midst of a dilemma as to the best thing to do in dealing with children having special requirements, after trying and trying to find "the answer" or "a way," the parent or clinician interacting with the child sometimes would do well simply to *imagine* the possibilities; even better would be to imagine them together, and to go on from that point toward fruition of the imagined. Is it not true that we define ourselves as much by our imaginings or make-believe as by our more worldly actions? To imagine is to envision other possibilities, other places, processes, and relationships, other ways of living. But to imagine may mean our bringing to a conscious awareness what *could* be, but is not; what one may desire but does not see the possibility of attaining; plus, what one wishes to struggle for, even in the face of adversity.

It is this very behavior—imagining—that one may note a profound lack of in some severely handicapped persons. The parents of an autistic girl, as described by Clara Park in her book, *The Siege,* noticed the girl's lack of interest in *future* experience. One day, as they watched Elly move slowly through the hundreds of odd physical activities that were typical before she could settle down to the pleasant experience of school, the father suddenly realized that a sense of *purpose* was missing. The parents reasoned that purpose entails drive, but that the critical ingredient is the capacity to *imagine,* to bring to mind what is not immediate and concrete, and to act in relation to it. These parents attributed Elly's simplicity of mind, the emptiness of her horizons, to her lack of imagination. It's absence was reflected in many other ways, including her unusual absence of fear. She could not, they reported, be brought to fear traffic; she never looked both ways before crossing without being reminded; when she did look, she "looked without looking." In one way Elly knew that vehicles can hurt—she was once struck by a truck—but she could not *imagine the possibility,* then act accordingly.

As parents and workers we sometimes, on the other hand, imagine possibilities that lie beyond our grasp and our child's. Hopefully, we do not do so chronically. Most of us try to find the intersection of reality and dream, fact and fancy, the place where imagination and earth-bound things metamorphose into a creative act that turns a hope for the future into a fact of the past. Others of us imagine only woe—of course, even imagined woes bring pain; it has often been noted that most of our troubles do not happen, but our anticipation that they might constitutes most of our troubles. And so imagination, too, is a double-edged sword; if in our imaginings we get hurt too often, we may—at least for a time—resist imagining at all. Perhaps the mother of five children, three of whom had significant learning disabilities, made a point when she said:

Our dream-child will never be. Every parent has a dream-child, but eventually they have only a real child.

Occasionally, imagination takes the form of reverie-like associations as in the following instance, my recollection of one mother's recording in her clinical diary:

I look at my son as he sleeps. His athetotic twisting is now stilled. He is motionless, calm, quite normal-looking. Why do those demon tremors, those writhings and jerkings nearly always present otherwise, disappear in sleep? Is there in this phenomenon the secret of a cure? . . . He seems now like a statue—did I sculpt this? (Did the hand of the potter go awry?) How beautiful he is. I contemplate him deeply. I try to sweep all thought away, to see him for himself alone and not as society has taught me to see him, or in comparison with other children, or in terms of my hopes and expectations, but *only to see him for himself alone*. When I am able to better achieve this clear experiencing—this pure sensing of his reality—he shines more brightly. I experience his true essence. And during my total attention I seem to become, for that moment, selfless and perhaps more completely in a state of oneness with my child. I feel somehow wonderful—transported beyond the everyday minutiae to which I typically react and even help to create. In this quiet moment of mind-wandering, I have broken out of the walls of my usual world. It is as though I am seeing him, and perhaps part of myself, for the first time—or for the last.

In traditional Japanese painting the artist is required, when painting a tree, to *feel* the strength of its branches, to *feel* the grace of the opening blossom, to "become one" with the subject so as to experience it in the most complete and natural way. One is reminded of how frequently master painters gaze upon the same objects without ever tiring of them in their efforts to discover something new in them. Edward Steichen for many years photographed a particular shadblow tree near his home: "Each time I look at that tree, those pictures, I find something new there. Each time I get closer to what I want to say about that tree." Parents who bring devoted love to their children and to each other bring that openness and sense of wonderment shown by children in the typical spontaneity and fascination with which they meet the world. This is creative perception; its mate is imagination.

As I stare into the fire beside me, staring for a long time, surrendering to its magic, I surrender to nature's apparently irrational, oddly confused formations, and it somehow produces in me a feeling of harmony with the forces symbolized by the phenomena. In stoking the fire, I rekindle and build the flame higher. But I also cause the fire to consume its source and itself. Even though it be for a noble purpose, why must creation be accompanied by destruction? To see differently, I must relinquish old ways of seeing; to establish new relationships, I must give up some of the old and perhaps familiar; to create a new self, I must in some way abandon my old self.

Just so, the mother who surrendered herself to the sleeping form of her child had called forth from her depths a strange and wondrous sensation that she could not quite express, yet could not deny. In so losing ourselves, we sometimes find ourselves—we invent ourselves anew. These interludes must be like those we experience during moments when we are most loving and creative. Nor do we need always to have others share our experience. Persons who imagine the possibilities and give in to occasional mind-drifting may need no accompaniment. They perhaps know that they have a few friends who would approve if they were present.

SOLOING

The nightingale I know,
Blames not the cuckoo's song.
If I sing not like thee,
Thou sayst I do wrong.

Angelus Silesius, The Cherubinic Wanderer
(16th century)

When a parent with a special child becomes widowed, the effects may be more poignant and more complex than in a marital situation in which there are no children or in which only nonhandicapped children exist. Laurie, a publicity specialist for a recording company, was left with two preteen children, one of whom was severely learning-impaired:

I was angry for awhile, not only in general, but at my husband for dying and leaving me alone with all of this responsibility. His passing left me without any money, and I was terrified—no insurance, nothing—we lived that way. But, as Lynne Caine, who wrote *Widows* said, "They gave us lemons so I made lemonade!" I also concluded I was temporarily not responsible, and didn't make a major decision for a year. Gradually, my life achieved a new pattern.

Jodie, an elementary school teacher, was left with a thirteen-year-old daughter with cerebral palsy:

My toughest job was taking the place of her father. My daughter felt that half her world had been taken from her. "You can get another husband, Mom, but I can never have another father." Then, too, she felt some resentment because she thought she had been left out of being told how ill her father really was. My work had been a saver for me, and somehow we seem closer together—she's much more pleasant to be with—complains far less, asks how I'm doing. . . .

182

Diane, all of whose children had grown up and left home except for her seventeen-year-old retarded daughter, shared her feelings with our counseling group while discussing her reaction to her husband's sudden death:

Speaking selfishly, what I miss most is having someone around who loves me, who cares. My daughter has *me,* although I'm beginning to wonder and worry more about our future. Neither my husband nor I had close relatives. We loved each other very much. I miss him. But my daughter, in her own way, I think, misses him more. Something's missing from her life. Anyway, I don't intend to sit around. I intend to get a job, and we'll travel a lot. We'll have lots of people in—I love to cook, and Sally loves company. Still, loneliness is the biggest problem. Sally, thank goodness, still has her friends, but I, well, here it is Saturday and another night at home.

Joan, when her husband died, was left responsible for a retarded daughter and two sons. She began working as a waitress to support the family, and within a year or so was thinking again of marriage:

But if I'm going to get really serious with any man—as much as I want to be with someone—he must be able to set up a relationship with my children. Let's face it. That's a tall order to ask of any man. I just may not make it. I do all right most of the time, but I may be kidding myself. I'm not as certain of myself as I'd like to be—my coping ability—my—our—future. I'm not getting any younger. Sometimes it's scarey.

Similar statements, of course, are heard in instances of divorce—which itself can constitute a little death:

In my life two of my most natural instincts have taken a pounding. One was my instinct to love a man in marriage, and that was shattered by his not being faithful to me. The second was my instinct to have a child, and Peter was born—brain-injured—two months after I left my husband. For two years I could not love—anything. I was angry, resentful, absolutely frustrated, asking about the meaning of life, was it worth it, the whole thing. But my best friend—and you've got to have a friend—she came by one day and just asked me if I could meet the test of believing this to be God's will and accepting that and expressing my love. Somehow I did, and It's been easier since to love Peter more and more, and, at the same time, I feel better toward other people, too, including other men. So my instincts were battered, but the maternal instinct, well—I guess none of my instincts were dealt a deathblow. But for a period of time I was in bad shape.

Divorce or separation can be terribly painful. In the clinical situation, if there is unusual stress in the parent, it is not at all typically related to the special child—that is, the child may be as much a concern as previously and perhaps a bit more, but the major areas of stress usually relate to factors such as inadequate income, unfulfilled financial expectations ("I thought he would at least support us"), less desirable residential situation, a lack of leisure time (or an inability to enjoy it), and, too often, an apparently increased tendency toward physical illness which is probably related to greater stress and a reduced capacity to deal with stress.

The little world that I had built for myself had become a hell. I even think my despair had become my passion. I started to snap out of it when my old professor said to me one day when I visited him, "You remind me of Kafka. He avoided people not because he wanted to live quietly but because he wanted to die quietly. You're so preoccupied with yourself," he said, "that you respond to nothing at all." It took me a long time to come back. Even though my marriage failed, and my kids didn't turn out well, that doesn't mean I failed as a human being. But for a long time I thought I had. The interest of a few concerned and loving persons pulled me back to life.

To live in a state of utter isolation, to feel cut off from all social nourishment, left to oneself alone, is to be hurt, sorely beset. What power is it that enables a person to fight off the terrible necessity to pull back on one's faith, hopes, dreams, or caring to the point of depression represented by the hurting situation? What is it that enables one to live rather than die, to reach out rather than withdraw, to exercise will and strength rather than give in to weakness, to have joy triumph over sorrow, love over hate? Each of us has the answer, if we can but tap our own deepest resources; only each of us, alone, ultimately can answer for ourselves.

Partnerships sometimes fail. Lucky are the partners who are eager for the other's growth, who hold respect for the other's unique and individual personality, who are happy rather than threatened by the other's triumphs, who *affirm* the other, granting full right to the other's personhood.

Now that I've married again, I've begun, with my husband's help, to cut down on that sense of duty that hangs around my neck like an albatross. I don't always have to be with my children. I've struggled, but I'm preserving some remnants of independence and "me-ness." I don't go back to "before" as much. Partly it's because now I have someone to share with, discuss things, work together—I escaped.

Even in an ideal partnership there is some pain. The commitment to marriage and children is sometimes—let us say it—simply a nuisance. We often put ourselves out to a great extent in terms of our own interests or wishes, simply because we know the other has need of us. In truth, no couple can converge in complete harmony for more than a few peak moments. The basis of a good relationship is that two people can be together comfortably fairly often, with each being a supportive counterpoint for the other, without loss of individuality. But even in the healthy and loving merger, there must be separateness as well.

Even the healthiest of us now and then requires privacy— the simple right to be left alone. Our public lives are all too public, especially if our child has a publicly observable impairment. Our children require privacy, too, the solitude that allows a dream to take shape, the reverie that may lead to discovery, the time to look within, to ponder and wonder, to work out decisions. This is the solitude that replenishes, as the mother of a hyperactive blind child stated:

I dearly love good conversation, but quiet solitude can be so much more eloquent. When I'm with my son, my husband, or others, I try to be with them fully, but if I feel like being alone, I want to be entirely alone. Sometimes it's in a cathedral, or when listening to magnificent music. I simply *must* have some freedom to be myself for myself alone. I now know that, in an important way, I am more nearly myself when alone than I am when I'm with others—even those I love. It need not be a big occasion. Arranging my hanging plants can give me a sense of peace, a moment of inward attention.

One of the most spiritually nourishing books of our time is May Sarton's *Journal of a Solitude.* In that remarkable book she refers to another splendid one, Louis Lavelle's *La Mal et la Souffrance.* Both authors speak of their belief that solitude is one way toward communion. One can say that one begins to communicate with others as soon as one begins to communicate with oneself. Solitude can give a strong sense of inner responsibility, but it can also suggest the impossibility of being entirely self-sufficient. Such solitudes constitute in part a silent calling-out to solitudes like our own, to others with whom we sense a need to be in a communion.

Solitude can be sweet. But when it is continued for too long, solitude may mean an indescribable, unendurable kind of anguish; the unappeasable loneliness; the longing to find greater meaning in existence; the unending struggle with one's own nature. Parents react to being "alone" in various ways:

You make a mistake, Doctor, when you merely explain my behavior, or simply describe me, and then perhaps try to alter me for your own purposes, when you should try to *experience* me. Then we'll get somewhere.

I'm a realist. When you're left to raise your children alone, you've got to stop feeling sorry for yourself *soon*. The kids need me now more than ever. I make myself get out and talk with people. I ask for help and advice. I contact the agencies. I keep working at it. Most of all, I don't give up.

About all I can say about raising kids alone is don't cut them off. On some days you may want to lock yourself in your room, but don't cut them off.

I'm not too proud to ask my relatives and friends for help. Most of them appreciate being asked. They'd be hurt if you didn't.

God knows our separation is no bed of roses. But Nancy—she's always been an emotional handful anyway—she takes the simple view that if her daddy left, then he musn't have liked her, or why would he leave? And she *means* that. I don't know. Maybe my having to spend so much time taking care of her problems keeps me from going off the deep end myself.

It's easy to say, "Start up a new life." *He* can do it—go out to bars, meet people—he's free that way. But look at me. Stuck here with four kids. I can't just pick up and go like him. And he's more attractive to the opposite sex, too, because he's free of the kids. I'm not, and believe me it doesn't help my chances of finding somebody.

I think of parents who were alone because of a spouse's death or separation, those who had never been married or in a continuing relationship with a parental partner, those who were in a relationship but still felt unhappily isolated, and, finally, those who simply longed for moments of peaceful solitude or healing escape. When I think of those who managed their family situations best, these characteristics are the ones I associate with their success in raising a child with special needs:

1. They admitted and accepted their feelings openly.
2. They had the assistance of a caring, supportive person.
3. Some built a cluster of interested people into a mutual-support group for both themselves and their children.
4. They remembered to satisfy their own needs and were not merely responsive to the needs of others.
5. They held a belief in something to live for—a religious faith, a child, one's own personhood, some source of joy or beauty.

The mother of five children, three having significant special needs, spoke for many single parents when she said at one of our evening "open clinics":

Quite often people tell me how wonderful they think I am. But I am like that lady who said, "But I am the mother. If not I, who then, and if not now, when?" And usually there is really no response to that. I don't want admiration or pity for my "noble" behavior. I want our acceptance and understanding by more and more people, and more service from the society for people with handicaps. I think it is all right that some of the benefits of our taxes go not just to the taxpayer but to everyone. Parents can do a lot, but they can't always do everything alone.

Another single parent that evening made this forceful statement:

We deserve compensation for work done, for the devotion we've given. We don't deserve to isolate ourselves, to lose our old friends, to give up doing the little things that give us some pleasure. We love our children. We don't begrudge the care they need. But we have needs, too. We need to keep a balance in our own lives. People should respect that fact.

Life, even a blemished one, is a precious gift. The traditional Hebrew toast, *Le Chaim* ("to life") celebrates the gift of living—through pain and joy. In Thornton Wilder's play, *Our Town,* a young woman who has died has the chance to relive a single day of her life. She comes to realize that the apparently boring and uninteresting happenings of life can be sources of pleasure if one but looks for the joy: the beauty of flowers, the good smell of coffee brewing, a soothing hot bath, perhaps simply looking at or talking with another. It is a realization the living need to take to heart.

I have said this elsewhere: Nowhere that I know of has it ever been promised that life will be simple, easy, or free from pain and uncertainty. Parents—even single parents—of impaired children have a particular task, but also a special opportunity to become *more* fully human persons through relationships with their children, and their children through them. Special professionals have the very same opportunities. Many of us have concluded that the purpose of life is not to be forever happy, but to matter, to be productive in the deepest human sense, to be in a significant relationship with one or more persons. Happiness in this noble sense means fulfillment through helpful relationships with others, stretching the resources of our minds and hearts.

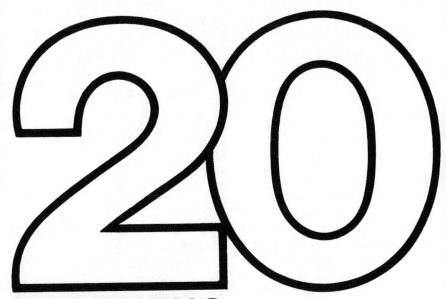

20
BEGINNING (AGAIN)

Every person born into this world
represents something new, something
that never existed before, something
original and unique. It is the
duty of every person to know . . .
that there has never been
anyone like him in the world, for
if there had been . . . there
would have been no need . . . to be
in the world. Every [person]
is a new thing in the world and
is called upon to fulfill his
particularity in the world.

Martin Buber (*Hasidism and Modern Man*
[New York: Harper Torchbooks, 1966], p. 139.)

Children are not only themselves; each is also the special point where all that is life and the world intersect, only once in a unique way, only once and no more. For this reason each child is important and, in fact, divine, a marvelous thing deserving of our finest respect and attention. Living by this view as parent or worker is rarely simple, however. There are days, even after years of interacting with special children, when one feels relatively more puzzled and less knowing about them. After years of investment, we may feel that we have not caught up with the scheme of things. This might be rather discouraging for the ardent seeker, until we shift our focus into a perspective where we once more see that it is the working through as much as finding simple answers that count in our progress with special children. It is in this sense that life is a search, a journey of self-discovery through relationship with others—especially others who have special need of us. In the words of Cervantes, "The road is always better than the inn." And in our search, while we may be bruised or even battered from time to time, there will be surprising moments of contentment or joy; John Masefield touched on the matter when he wrote, "I have seen flowers come in stony places,/And kindness done by men with ugly faces." It takes quite an effort to bring our best to the journey; but the enjoyment of beauty, the achievement of goodness and efficiency, the enhancement of life and its variety—these constitute the harvest.

What happened to us happened. But that is the past, and the past has gone. We can still live fully; before us lies the future, which we can shape.

So spoke the parent of a blind child who had known times when a sense of the tragic seemed engulfing. The tragic sometimes spells out the limits of being human, but it also teaches us human possibility. Even when life is poor and brutish, it need not be meaningless. Human beings may be crushed, but the human spirit endures.

He was like a lovely angel at times, yet in the very next moment he could break my heart. Somehow, we all survived.

It is hard at such times not to think we should get all we ourselves can out of life rather than trying so much to make the lives of others happy. Some parents, however, need encouragement in learning the difference between mature self-regard and selfishness. So many find it difficult to be good to themselves.

One may give all one has to give to a child, be creative in one's behavior, yet not always evoke an appropriate response. Still, the greatest living is in *mutually* creative relationship with another. However, a relationship need not always be mutual to be essentially creative; where one's creative impulse has taken hold in another, the originator somehow adds a new dimension to the self. One begins with oneself, but does not end with oneself.

Thomas Proctor, one of Wellesley College's most beloved professors, in a "Swan Song" he wrote for the college just before his death at age ninety-two, stated: "Life—time itself—they are a perpetual dying. But what we contribute survives us, entering into a stream of history; a new factor in the making of a universe that is never made, but always in the making. The meaning of life is thus to be found in its creativity."

Every human being is inherently great—and ultimately unfathomable. May we respect all persons, no matter how imperfect, as though they were gods unknown to us in their present state. This will require a faith and a sense of wonder in us that perhaps we have forgotten. I am reminded of the following story: Picasso, during World War II, was viewing an exhibition of English children's drawings compiled by Sir Herbert Read. He spent a long time looking at the pictures. Finally he said, "When I was the age of these children, I could paint like Raphael. It took me many years to learn how to paint like these children." Part of the responsibility of each adult is to rediscover this unaffected way of relating to the world, of living life every minute with all the passion of a lover or a discoverer.

While visiting the parents of an eighteen-year-old retarded young man recently, I noticed a poster in his bedroom with this quotation from Camus:

Don't walk in front of me—
  I may not follow.
Don't walk behind me—
  I may not lead.
Walk beside me—
  And just be my friend.

I asked the mother, a former student of mine and a social worker, what she would say in a few words as a personal statement about counseling parents of exceptional children; a few days later I received in the mail her statement:

All human beings can learn from one another and have a capacity and desire to share experiences with one another. No one individual has all the answers, and this includes any "expert." Parents want to learn to be better at parenting, want the best for their children, have concerns that they consider unique to them (which may or may not be unique), have concerns for the health and safety of their children, want their children to become successful adults, want to improve as parents, have difficulty in opening up to professionals, find it easier to communicate with other parents, know more about their child than any one else, and have the ultimate responsibility for their children.

Parents of handicapped children have a sense of failure as a result of producing a handicapped child. They need support and reassurance in their role as parents; need to know that it is okay to have both good and bad feelings about their handicapped kids; need to understand that they as well as the child are growing and changing; have the need to nurture their child while recognizing its striving for independence and separation in its growth to adulthood; and yet need to accept and understand the limitations the handicap may place on these goals. Most of all, the special knowledge and expertise of the parent should be recognized by the professional.

Participating in the lives of special children is frustrating and fascinating. We play many roles in the process, and interwoven are the countless distractions that are part of every life. It is quite a trick to keep from scrambling the roles, to make the quick shift from one to the other—caretaker, teacher, listener, friend. Every individual's situation is unique, and it is a lot of work to keep a healthy balance. Every parent or professional lives, works, and stays vital as long as there is response with spirit and some success to the challenges. If we stop responding, we die. We stop responding only if we relinquish the will and the strength to persevere, to make our own decisions, and to abide by our own true conscience. We work with what we have and what we believe. There will be doubts, but doubt will be used as a springboard to more productive reasoning; it will not be merely a confusing factor, unsettling in its provocation of anxiety. Finally, at some point we may say, "Everything is worth knowing; perhaps this is the real reason for living."

The creative adult and the special child in the process of moving from creative insecurity toward increased actualization and fuller humanity are seeking a new kind of wholeness and integrity. The ultimate purpose of truly creative endeavor is to satisfy our human hunger for a sense of community with others. The dilemmas, the perils in the human condition, are real. We are beset by them—or we manage them—to the degree to which we understand and communicate with one another. We must use our gifts, be as authentic as we are capable of being, become better instruments for helping and being fully with one another. Perhaps we truly are but intermediaries through which passes all that we have met and by way of which, hopefully— and in the best sense—others are touched. This hunger for identification, for truly evolving as fully functioning individuals, and the urge to satisfy this hunger provide the impulse behind all creative effort, not only for the parent or worker, but for the special child as well.

We have run a considerable gamut of the human experience. Could we perhaps say in conclusion that we emerge like Jacob from his wrestling—stumbling and bruised but having heard from time to time the voice of an angel?

Begin!

INDEX